HOME IS THE DESERT

HOME I

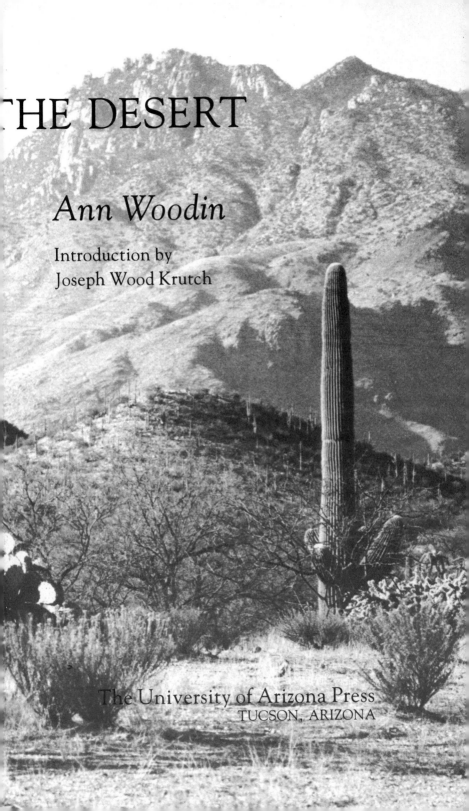

THE DESERT

Ann Woodin

Introduction by
Joseph Wood Krutch

The University of Arizona Press
TUCSON, ARIZONA

About the Author

ANN WOODIN began wintering in Tucson with her parents in 1937. After graduating from Wellesley College, she settled in the Tucson area as the wife of Bill Woodin, herpetologist and desert ecologist who was director of the internationally known Arizona-Sonora Desert Museum for almost twenty years. Ann's household, described in *Home Is the Desert,* came to include not only a husband and four sons but also an assortment of animals both wild and domestic. Her second book, *In the Circle of the Sun,* is based on the family's year-long camping trip through the Old World deserts between Calcutta and Casablanca. Her latest book is entitled *The Rule of Two.*

The author wishes to thank the following publishers for permission to quote selections in this book:

Dodd, Mead & Company, The Ryerson Press, and Ernest Benn Limited, for material from "The Spell of the Yukon" by Robert Service, reprinted from *The Complete Poems of Robert Service;* and Houghton Mifflin Company, for material from *Robinson Crusoe's Story* by Charles Carryl.

THE UNIVERSITY OF ARIZONA PRESS
First Printing 1984
Manufactured in the U.S.A.

Library of Congress Cataloging in Publication Data

Woodin, Ann.
   Home is the desert.

   Reprint. Originally published: New York : Collier Books, 1964.
   1. Desert fauna—Arizona.   2. Deserts—Arizona.
I. Title.
QL116.W66   1984   508.791   84-118
ISBN 0-8165-0857-7

To Bill
with love and appreciation

Contents

Contents

Introduction

Sometime during my first year in Tucson I was casually introduced to a young couple about to take off for the Galápagos. Little did I suspect (as the suspense novels so often put it) that they were presently to become one of the more important of the many reasons why I have never regretted my move to Arizona.

Readers of this book will come quickly to understand some, but by no means all, of the reasons why they are perfect companions for those of us who share their interests and attitudes. I know no one who takes fuller or more joyous advantage of precisely those special attractions which life in this region affords. Doing that means a good deal more than merely "liking nature" in some vague way. It means combining aesthetic appreciation and intelligent curiosity with something harder to define which I can only call an emotional rapport.

Mr. Woodin is a scientist first and also director of the increasingly famous Arizona-Sonora Desert Museum which is neither a botanical garden nor a zoo in the ordinary sense, but a unique institution which exhibits out of doors an extensive living collection of the plants and animals of the Sonoran desert. However he is not merely a scientist, because, unlike many scientists, he adds to a passion for accurate knowledge an emotional commitment and sheer joy in the great privilege of being able to participate imaginatively in the whole adventure of life, non-human as well as human, on this earth. His author-wife is a perfect complement because she not only shares his delight in the things which delight him but is also, though she would not call herself a scientist, full of scientific curiosity as well as of the other mental and temperamental characteristics necessary to make the life they lead a deeply satisfying one.

Together they explore, collect, camp, and (to mention last what is perhaps the chief subject of her book) care for and love the procession of often improbable animals which they do not so much "keep" as permit to live with them and the four sons whom Bill (who loves to tease his very philoprogenitive wife) sometimes pretends to consider less interesting than the animals the boys take for granted as companions.

Theirs is the only house I have ever had the privilege of frequenting where a full-grown bobcat may casually leap into your lap to have his belly rubbed. In fact the only other person I have so much as heard of who "lived with" animals more intimately is the nineteenth century English naturalist Charles Watterton, who went to the possibly eccentric extreme of always kissing his chimpanzee good night and on at least one occasion slept in the bed with a boa constrictor.

How all this works out Mrs. Woodin will describe better and more fully than I can. But there are two things I feel I should say which are to some extent left unsaid. The first of these is that the reader is wrong if he suspects that all this "togetherness" must make for a certain messiness. Mr. Woodin is one of the most resolutely orderly persons I have ever known and his wife is a close second. Add to this the fact that she is also effortlessly and efficiently energetic: everything is in its place and there is never any careless make-do. I know of no household which is "better run" and I know many childless and petless homes which are a great deal less so. The Woodins are charming hosts even to nature haters, who can dine there without ever suspecting that there are snakes in the study, a tarantula in a glass cage, a bobcat in the children's quarters, and perhaps a coyote or a wolf with the dogs somewhere in the surrounding out-of-doors.

The other possible suspicion which I would like to dispel is that the Woodins are people-haters because they are animal-lovers, or that there is anything fanatical, sentimental, or monomaniacal about either them or the lives they lead. The real cream of the jest in the anecdote Mrs. Woodin tells about how they were once photographed in the wild by two lady tourists who took them for wild mountain folk is that they could easily be mistaken at a dinner party for—well, for the kind of people you meet at the more elegant dinner parties. Please, when you read, do not think of flat-heeled shoes and blue jeans as Mrs. Woodin's only costume or tiresome theories on animal behavior as her only conversation. She is gay, humorous, and knowing about a great many things which have nothing to do with natural history. To describe primarily one side of the Woodin's varied life, a publisher insufficiently averse to cliché titles might have been tempted to call her book: *Living with Animals Can Be Fun.*

JOSEPH WOOD KRUTCH

Acknowledgments

Obviously a book is the sum of many parts. To the following University of Arizona professors I wish to extend my thanks for their help with certain of those parts: Dr. George D. Butler, Jr., for having successfully persuaded me that not all "bugs" are bugs; Dr. Charles T. Mason, Jr., for having brought some order out of the mysteries of plant nomenclature; Dr. Joe T. Marshall, Jr., who patiently led me through a few of the intricacies of the bird world; and Dr. William L. Nutting, who revealed to me the marvels of the termite.

I wish also to thank Stephen H. Congdon, who sorted out various rock layers and other geological puzzles; Julian D. Hayden, for his help with the archaeology of the Pinacate; Alexander J. Lindsay, Jr., research associate at the Museum of Northern Arizona, and its Director, Dr. Edward B. Danson, both of whom brought to life the rock pictures, pottery shards, and crumbling walls of the long-gone Anasazi Indians of the Glen Canyon region; and the staff of the Arizona-Sonora Desert Museum, particularly its Director who, among many things, benevolently but firmly monitored my adjectives and superlatives.

I'm indebted to the following for their photographic contributions: E. Tad Nichols, Mervin W. Larson, Melanie Walker, Lewis Wayne Walker, LeRoi Russel, and Carl Holzman.

And, lastly, I want to thank Joseph Wood Krutch, whose vision all along has supplied integral spark; my sons, who supplied much of the material, consciously or otherwise, and a good deal of its joy; and my editor, Peter Ritner, pin-sticker, watchdog, and guardian angel.

ANN WOODIN

1

The Walk

WERE you to fly high over the southwestern part of our country, you would look down on a lean and frugal land, burnt by the sun, creased by mountains, fissured by canyons and empty river beds. For the most part the land is bleached and dry, but you would see occasional patches of black lava, and of dark green marking the highest mountains and plateaus. The wide sky is made for eagles to soar in, and could you listen you would hear them scream. It is a noble land, fierce and unyielding, and the eye becomes used to looking at things far away.

In the winter the Pacific winds slide over the mountains, sometimes bringing with them rain. In the burning summers other winds blow in from the Gulf of Mexico to inflate huge thunder clouds. When these burst, the land is briefly cooled and the fleeting grass grows. And the air is so clear and weightless as to be nonexistent, and the sun feels close and hot.

We call this land a desert though to some this may not seem to be altogether true. An Italian expert on the Sahara, come to study our Arizona desert, stepped off the plane, looked around him, and said, "But where is the desert?" Though very different from the barren sand dunes of the Sahara, our cactus- and shrub-covered landscape is a desert nevertheless. Why? Because it possesses certain necessary features: heat, low humidity, and comparatively little rainfall. Our summer months enjoy an average daily high of around 100 degrees and a low in the 70's; our average yearly rainfall is eleven inches, most of which falls either in summer cloudbursts or more gently during the winter months; and in the middle of the day our humidity often falls below 5 per cent.

We live in a forty-acre square of this desert, near Tucson, Arizona, a square dissected by a seemingly undesertlike stream lined with trees—not a dry wash that runs only when it rains, but almost a real stream with water in it more than half the year. This is one of the most pleasant of the many surprises with which the desert abounds.

Close to the north of us are the Santa Catalina Mountains. They present to us an ever-changing backdrop of light and color on which to look, and in their heights our stream is born. Farther away, to the east, are the round-backed Rincons; to the west, farther away still and hidden by the intervening hills, are low, jagged, volcanic peaks, drawn on the horizon as a child might draw them. Between these and ourselves lies the city. To it we are connected by our dirt road that climbs up and down a few hills until it merges with the official black pavement. At the end of this umbilical cord we swing somewhat apart. But we are grateful that, unlike an umbilical cord, our road does not furnish all of our needs.

In the middle of our desert square, on the side of a hill and overlooking the narrow valley which shelters the stream, spreads our adobe brick house. It pushes out untidily in every direction like a giant amoeba. In this house besides my husband and me live four "commonly cultivated and freely escaping" boys (to use a botanical phrase), a German shepherd, a black and white cat, a natural procession of bobcats, and, for seasoning, an occasional wolf or coyote or peccary or raven, an owl or two, many snakes, lizards, tarantulas, ground squirrels, and one alligator. This little world, as every other, wheels through the years with varying degrees of smoothness, events as well as the changing seasons marking the passing time.

Because of our situation with the hills about us, our eye takes in not the whole expansive range of mountains, but is focused on a few peaks, ridges, and canyons; and in our small valley our eye is drawn to the one tree, the one flower, the one rock, rather than to the whole macrocosm of nature. We find our domain eminently satisfactory, and by osmosis it has seeped into the fiber of our sons. A child's imagination thrives in protected nooks and crannies which he can explore and people as his fancy moves him: a hollow of a tree where a dwarf might live, a pool where Ratty hides, a hole in the bank just right for a hobbit. In a nook he can build himself a fort, with a flag flying over it and a piece of canvas for a door. And as he finds an arrowhead partly buried in the sand he catches a brief vision of the past, when the land he lives in was wild and unhandled and those who preceded him were content that it should be so. Not long ago Michael, our nine-year-old, announced at the dinner table: "I wouldn't like to live all hunched up in a city like a grain of sand on the beach. I just couldn't bear it."

But from behind our hills we can hear the city stirring as it creeps forward, and I sometimes wonder if, as Thoreau said, "most men . . . do not care for nature and would sell their share in all of her beauty for a given sum."

Since World War II Tucson, like so many other southwestern cities, has been in the merciless grip of a population explosion, growing from 30,000 to 300,000. Its Chamber of Commerce enthusiastically describes desert living on the one hand, urging people to come to Tucson to enjoy it, and on the other hand it defines progress as a continually expanding city and encourages the developer who sees the desert only as a foundation for more houses. The once small sleepy cowtown with its sprinkling of health-seekers and winter visitors has been submerged under a deluge of neon signs, car lots, and trailer courts. Outlying cattle ranches convert to guest ranches and then to real-estate. Walking along its downtown streets where one is just as likely to hear Spanish as English, one is reminded that somewhere hidden under all the urban ugliness are the bones of a long and colorful history, for two hundred years ago Tucson was a walled presidio connected to Spain's great empire to the south by a feeble thread, the Camino Real—now called Main Street!

Life here can be essentially the same as anywhere else: a round of cocktail parties, bridge and golf games, civic board-meetings, and university lectures. Last week we could have attended a symposium on the significance of head-nodding in turtles, and tomorrow we shall attend the opening of the new air terminal. Ours is a remarkably polyglot city, its winter flood of visitors from all parts of the world flavoring it in unexpected ways. Less "provincial" than most cities of its size, it is as necessarily provincial as every city, large or small, for man does not comfortably belong to the world, but rather to a tiny piece of it—a city, as did the Athenians, a patch of land, as do we.

Before me as I sit writing is a window looking north. Outside it is late November, and the strong white morning light has smoothed out the rough mountains and hills so that they are flat and even. This dazzling light, that is such a marvel to the newcomer, has also leached out their color. Most of the day the sun spreads the land with a luminous white wash that diffuses not only color but form and substance. The desert belongs to the sun: it shimmers as the sun shimmers, sears as the sun sears, and it flames red as the flaming sun drops behind the mountains. Nothing is between us and the sun. We are tethered to it.

Close at hand is a mesquite tree, and a Gila woodpecker is hopping about in it, busily stuffing dried bean pods into cracks in the bark. He has been doing this for weeks now, and I'm beginning to wonder if it hasn't become an obsession so that he cannot stop any more than a squirrel can stop piling nuts into holes.

As I sit looking out I try to shed the cloak of familiarity and see what is spread before me as if for the first time. Then it is that the desert turns to me a forgotten face, the wintry visage of an

4

invincible old man, so old that it has linked itself again with the newborn and is therefore ageless. Gray, unadorned, and peculiarly static, it lies in undreaming stillness. So terribly aloof, so terribly impassive is the desert that here, more than anywhere else except perhaps on the ocean, one is overwhelmingly conscious of the total indifference of nature.

An old tradition defines the desert as a wasteland, a place where only scorpions, deadly serpents, and hermits live. Thus it symbolizes the complete abnegation of the world's Paphnutiuses, who have withdrawn from humanity and seek salvation through the hideous mortification of the flesh that is implied by living in the desert. A less esoteric attitude toward the desert is embodied by such adjectives as hot, dry, hostile, and lifeless. This is how most people who reside in more benign surroundings think of it and why they naturally recoil from it. Once this was how I thought of it.

I remember, when I was eleven, looking at our New England meadow bordered by tangled woods and trying to imagine the desert that was to be the goal of our first trip west. I had a well-formed picture of what I would find: quantities of sand; and like the Walrus and the Carpenter, I too thought that "if this were only cleared away it would be grand." As the actual Arizona desert skimmed by the train window I thought how dismally bare it all was, how open and empty. Later I realized that this effect is due to the fact that the existing growth, though plentiful enough, is small-leaved and low to the ground. Because one can usually see over it, the eye has a tendency to scan the desert. It hurries on until it is brought up sharply against the framing mountains, whether close by or fifty miles away. My next impression, and an enduring one, was that of prickliness. Everything was covered with spines. As a friend of ours put it: "The most often heard sound in the desert is 'ouch!'" And finally, as I looked on what seemed to be a wholly unsympathetic waste of rock, sand, and dried up prickly plants, I thought the desert was dead. It was silent and nothing

5

Our view to the north: mesquite and saguaro cactus are in the right foreground, and the Santa Catalina Mountains are in the background

moved. It might just as well have been the inanimate surface of an unknown planet. Up to then I had put my arms around my surroundings, hugging the fields and woods to me as I might have hugged a cat, but this sharp-elbowed, abrasive landscape made me shrink, and gingerly I stepped out into it.

Having been nurtured on green and shade, the love of the desert came to me slowly, for it is a hard-mind place, not a soft-skin place, and concealed in its openness. You cannot stroke it as you would a meadow, you cannot dissemble, nor are there corners in which to hide. You can only fling wide your arms, sprawl on the nail-bed, let the skin be punctured and the mind ooze out to be bleached in the sun. Then you will find yourself standing in the light, miraculously whole and as skeletal as the desert itself. In its qualities of severity and reserve, in its harmony of line and color, in its abstraction of design, lies an uncompromising formality. No other scene achieves this to such a degree. Once met on its own terms it evokes a curious tranquility and composure.

No, the desert cannot be fought successfully; and to join it one must come to know it, and to know it one must walk in it. It is then that the desert begins to stir, and we gradually find ourselves in the comforting company of other living and warm-blooded creatures.

We shall go out the front door and up the slight rise to the crest of the hill behind our house. Hugh, the youngest, has joined us, and of course the dog. It is late afternoon. There are many ways to walk. You can walk just to get somewhere; you can walk to look for something; you can walk in order to simply breathe in all that is around. Hugh and his father are looking for things and I am breathing. But they also are breathing as I am looking.

The mountains now are purplish in the softening light, and the lowering sun, profiling their ridges against the leeward shadows, pleats them crisply like a paper accordion. No longer cardboard flat, they now sit squat and heavy on the desert floor. These are not the smooth, fleshy mountains of my eastern childhood. They are gaunt and tough, with their ribs showing, and their sinews. It was yesterday that the earth cracked and these pushing shoving mountains were forced up, lifting the dry metamorphosed bottom of the Paleozoic sea high into the air. Slowly over the ages they shook it off their backs, covering their feet with foothills of rubble and filling the valley beyond. Because they are young and because of the lack of continually eroding rainfall, our mountains look new and strong and bony.

Above us the sky is bright, clear, and empty except for a red-tailed hawk floating about in the sun-drenched blueness, looking for a meal. The buzzards have abandoned this realm and have gone south for the winter. The boys call them the desert garbage collectors, and Hugh once became quite upset when he first learned that they leave in October not to return until March. "Who is going to eat up all the dead things now?"

If we are not to stumble into a cactus we must direct our attention to the immediate surroundings. Here up on this hill there are no trees, but down in the washes on either side of the hill thorny mesquite and catclaw grow. We call them trees even though they are shrubby ones, spreading out quickly from a short trunk. The mesquites are hard and wiry with dark twisting branches, evoking when leafless the mood of a Chinese print. Now, even though it is almost December, they still hold on to their small gray-green acacia-like leaves, though the long yellow seed-pods have fallen. At home Hugh has a boxful of them. He occasionally takes one out and rattles it. I think he also eats them. Our pediatrician says not to worry, for they are rich in protein. The catclaw, as the name implies, has grasping curved thorns. It belongs to the mimosa group of the pea family, as does the mesquite, but it is even shrubbier, with smaller leaves. Each leaf is no larger than a grain of rice.

An endlessly fascinating thing about the desert is the remarkable ways in which plants and animals alike have evolved to successfully endure its rigors. Catclaw and mesquite are typical products of the desert lowlands. The smallness of their leaves helps to reduce the loss of moisture that is so vital to arid living, and the long tap root reaches down for the dampness more likely to be present there than in the hills. Perhaps the most dramatic example of desert adaptation in trees is the palo verde, two Spanish words meaning "green stick." This handsome tree has no need of any leaves at all, though it does sprout tiny ones during the summer. Its bark carries on photosynthesis, usually the function of the leaves, and therefore it is green. The most common species of palo verde grows in the foothills, but since we live in more of a lowland situation, we have very few of them.

John looking at a cactus wren nest in a staghorn cholla cactus

Around us on the hill are many brownish-green, bunchy shrubs that are called creosote, though locally they are often known as greasewood. Their shiny little leaves, which they keep all year, are covered with a secretion that not only helps reduce transpiration but when wet inundates the air with a distinct and pungent odor. It is easy to tell when it has rained in this desert even if one has not seen or heard it, and when I am elsewhere during a rain, the absence of the accustomed odor makes the air seem dull and flat. The creosote are still covered with diminutive gray, furry seed balls that come as close as the desert can come to one of my childhood favorites, the pussy willow. Some of the branches of the shrub beside me have been recently chewed off by a porcupine who has wandered down from the mountains on a visit.

The low sun turns the long glistening spines of the cholla to silver. A cactus wren flies out from one, startling Hugh, who is close to it. We see hidden among the spines the entrance to this bird's winter resting nest. Several different kinds of cholla are scattered about and each is a more fearsome tangle of needles sprouting from a fat short trunk than the last. By far the most unpleasant of these is the jumping cholla whose joints disengage at the slightest touch. This plant—also known as the chain-fruit cactus because the fruits do not function as such but may remain in position each succeeding year, forming long chainlike append-ages—reproduces from the joints taking root as they fall on the ground. To my mind the handsomest cholla is the staghorn, so named because of an imagined resemblance to branching antlers, an excellent example of poetic fancy carried to an extreme.

Cacti are interesting phenomena, native almost entirely to the New World, though the prickly pear and others have been transported far and wide. Believed to be an offshoot of the ances-tral rose, these plants have evolved in a most practical manner. As succulents their fleshy stems can store more water than is normally possible, and these, being green, can carry on photosynthesis as

Ocotillo plants

does the bark of the palo verde. In order to conserve water, they have forsaken leaves in favor of spines, which also serve as a protection against hungry mouths. This defensive device is not confined to cacti alone, but has been adopted by quite unrelated plants, the ocotillo for example. Along its branches one can see the transition from leaf to spine, beginning at the tip of the yearly new growth and progressing down to where the leaves have dropped off, leaving behind stems that dry up into thorns.

The ocotillo is a bizarre plant, a bundle of long (up to twenty feet) somewhat pliable sticks fanning out from a trunk so short as to be almost unnoticeable. Except for the new growth, these spindly branches are lined with thorns each of which, after a substantial rain, is concealed by a cluster of small leaves that turn the branches into furry green tails. In the spring each branch is tipped with a panicle of tiny bright-red flowers, like candle flames.

Underfoot the pebbly ground is somewhat springy and sprinkled with tufts of grass and small bushes, mostly zinnias and paper-flowers that even at this time of year are still gay with white or yellow flowers. Hugh is gathering the smoothest and most brightly colored stones that he can find. Sometimes he will find a gray piece of gneiss with both a flake of mica and a tiny ruby-red garnet imbedded in it, or perhaps a rock with both green and orange lichens clinging to its surface. The lichen will elicit a few remarks from his father on this most ancient plant—not a plant at all, but a miraculous symbiotic combination of two, a fungus and an alga, living together to their mutual benefit . . . "just as do your mother and father!" concludes my husband with a flourish. "Which of you is the fungus?" asks Hugh.

We pass a saguaro cactus. This particular one is large, nearly forty feet high with seven arms. Scientists are evasive about stating the ages of these cacti, but it is probably over 150 years old. Hugh has found a small saguaro nearby, growing under the sheltering shade of a mesquite tree. It is less than one foot high, which may represent some fifteen years' effort. The child is impressed and

PHOTO BY MERVIN W. LARSON

Elf owl in a saguaro cactus

thinks well of himself, who is so much larger after only half the time.

The saguaro, which occurs only in the Sonoran desert, is perhaps the most spectacularly grotesque of all our desert flora. It is ribbed like an accordion, and like an accordion it expands and contracts, but due to water rather than air. Having had an unusual amount of late summer rain, the saguaros are fat and swollen. They may weigh as much as one hundred pounds per foot. Two members of *Life* Magazine's staff once conducted an experiment on one of our saguaros. They watered it for days with a garden hose in hopes that a before-and-after picture would reveal a dramatic change in its girth. The saguaro expanded but not enough to fulfill the exigencies of the press.

Here we have very few saguaros, but closer to the mountains they cover the sides of the foothills like giant fingers. Back-lighted by a low-lying sun, their strangeness is accentuated, and I think I will never be able to look at them and feel as if they and I belong to the same world. Whether they are old with many arms, or young with only a first arm beginning to sprout halfway up like a ridiculous bulbous nose, they are equally alien. I did not feel this way, though, until I actually saw one. Perhaps a child is more willing to accept the unusual when it is confined to a picture. Before arriving on the desert I carefully examined certain photographs in the *National Geographic* and thought the saguaro would make a suitable substitute for a tree, and being in that stage of life, I could hardly wait to try one out. Unfortunately the *National Geographic* pictures had merely shown the fluted trunk and arms and not the long spines.

We wander over to look at another saguaro. Last summer an elf owl, the world's smallest owl, nested in one of its holes. These deep holes, which the cactus lines with "scar tissue," making a sort of shoe (as it is called), are first pecked out by the Gila woodpecker for its own nest. When the woodpecker moves out, the owl or some other bird moves in. Now, however, the nest is empty, as its occupant has left for the south, but in all probability he will be back next spring.

All around us this afternoon is the usual intense stillness. It always gives me the feeling of suspension, that life has withdrawn and is peeking out from behind closed shutters. And this is partly true, for desert animals, like all animals, are shy. Because here cover is scarce in which to hide, they retreat down holes for protection.

Holes can lead one into an endless and fascinating field of conjecture and, if one is Lewis Carroll, into sublime adventure. Like unblinking black eyes they stare up at the passerby and challenge him. Hugh is crouched over a small one at this very moment and is calling to his father. It is a very neat round hole with webbing around the entrance. Here lives a wolf spider, the next biggest spider to the tarantula, though he bears little resemblance to it and belongs to an entirely different family. As his name indicates, he stalks his prey rather than sitting at home in his web waiting. We share our house with a number of these creatures and I do not disturb them, for my husband says that they will catch other "bugs" that I prefer even less.

Later on we see a number of ground squirrel holes whose doorways are littered with half-eaten barrel cactus fruit, which resembles miniature pineapples with a stuffing of black seeds. If we are really lucky we will come across a badger hole, or better still, one belonging to a coyote. By far the most common hole is that of the ant. In some live small black ants who around their entrances have made volcanoes of fluffy white grass seeds. In others live large, black, long-legged ants who have made much larger and more rounded volcanoes of gravel, the empty shells of mesquite seeds, and creosote leaves.

So life is far from absent in this desert of ours, only it has to be looked for. An occasional thrasher will call harshly from the top of a saguaro, doves will whir by on their way to roost in the trees along the stream, and migrating white-crowned sparrows will flitter about in a burst of activity before bedtime, much like young children. One might surprise a Harris ground squirrel, a chipmunk-like creature, at dinner. Or glimpse a pack rat scuttling around the outside of his house on one of his rare diurnal ventures, the house itself an unfriendly looking place, a mess of cholla cactus joints and sticks heaped in a sprawling prickly pear. Obviously what is homelike to a pack rat is very different from what is home-like to me, especially as this home of his may also be sheltering a rattlesnake. The latter is quite uninvited and will have retreated there in face of the cold weather to spend the winter. Snakes, as well as lizards, being cold-blooded, must be careful to keep them-selves in surroundings that are neither too cold nor too hot, hiber-nating in winter as well as retiring during the heat of summer days. And certainly we will see a jack rabbit, that long-legged, long-eared hare. It may be an antelope jack who will flash the white hairs on his rump first on one side and then on the other as he zigzags away from us, for what purpose no one knows.

Suddenly the quiet is shattered by the wild barking of the dog after a cottontail, and we catch sight of her on the side of the next hill, her tail waving madly. However, as usually happens, the

Hugh looking at a ground squirrel hole

rabbit goes off in one direction and the dog in another. I once watched a coyote give chase with the same results. He finally sat down exhausted and panted, his tongue hanging out, looking thoroughly dejected and not a little embarrassed. The dog is soon back to check on us, pausing to remove a cholla joint from her paw, a trick she neatly executes with her teeth, and off she goes again on another scent.

We work our way down the hillside towards the sandy wash. Hugh has found a red velvet ant, which is not an ant at all. It is a female mutillid wasp, wingless, with a formidable compensating sting, the reverse in both respects of her male consort. These furry insects come in several colors and multitudinous species, and as they scurry across the desert floor, they easily catch the eye. Some claim that their fur coats, acting as an insulation, enable them to withstand surprisingly high temperatures.

We thread our way down the narrow wash in and out of the mesquite and catclaw. We hear voices, and on rounding a bend we come upon the two middle boys on their hands and knees. John is collecting sand-rubies, actually garnets, which have been washed out of the crumbling rocks and are carried down into the river beds where they collect in pockets among the stones. With a magnet Michael collects magnetite granules that streak the sand with black. Like the shipwrecked members of the *Piccadilly Daisy*

> . . . we gather as we travel
> Bits of moss and dirty gravel
> And we chip off little specimens of stone;
> And we carry home as prizes
> Funny bugs of handy sizes
> Just to give the day a scientific tone.

The other two boys join us as we climb up to the top of the next hill and walk through the short dead grass left over from the summer rains. It is called "six-weeks needle grama"—"six weeks" because of its short summer life and "needle" because of its sharp seeds that pierce socks and trouser cuffs like needles. The grass has been flattened in certain spots, and we guess that the coyotes come here to rest and to look at the moon.

The sun is rapidly losing its ability to warm, and the cold is seeping up from the low places, which reminds us that it is time for supper. "Even if we didn't see any lizards," says Hugh, "it was a beautiful walk."

Not long after we close the door I hear our oldest son calling to us from outside. "Come look! Look at the sunset!" I glance out the window and see Peter on his horse silhouetted against the orange-red sky, a scene as timeless and uncorruptible as any pure and true cliché. People have long painted and photographed the western sunset, and yet it is never believed by those who have never seen it. Like a fiery flow of molten lava the blazing clouds spread out from where the sun has set, igniting the world it has left behind. The colors slowly soften and the sky becomes less galvanizingly spectacular but more pervasively beautiful. The mountains are numberless shades of pink, and the eastern horizon is lightly flushed as if a second sun were setting there. Everything echoes the fading color, sending it back and forth across the sky from mountain range to mountain range so that the world is filled with an endless variety of the original theme and we are blissfully drowned in the ending day.

There are other ways to see the desert: through the wondrously revealing eyes of such a naturalist-writer as Joseph Wood Krutch, through the startled eyes of the newly arrived Easterner, through the technical eyes of the scientist, through the eyes of small boys.

To the adult eye, to the adult spirit, the desert above all else is remote. We do not see it move; we do not hear it breathe. Insidiously it sends out this quality of reserve and aloofness to steal into our consciousness like smoke, where it stifles our senses in a luminous aura of passivity. Were we metaphysically inclined we would remember that appearances are no more reliable than shadows and we would await its onslaught, for the desert has no intention of staying comfortably outside the house. In our four boys the desert has found just the accomplices it needs to infiltrate our lives most effectively. I am still astonished at the pieces of desert to be found in their rooms and pockets. What a specific, surprising, and varied place their desert is!

I find large broken-down shoe boxes filled with rocks, all kinds of rocks, gathered because of their shape or color, because they display a fossil trilobite or the imprint of an ancient fern, because they are obsidian or are stained turquoise from copper; and boxes of Indian pottery found not far from the house at an old camping site, Hohokam pottery of the twelfth or thirteenth century. I find pill bottles half full of garnets and magnetite granules, bits of mica wrapped up in cotton, a treasured piece of fool's gold. Praying mantis egg cases, cocoons, and mud-dauber nests are kept in jars, for they may unexpectedly hatch, or at any rate, that is the hope. I find a cottontail's cotton tail, several snake skins, a bird nest, mesquite beans, sycamore seed balls, devil's claws, a few dried gourds, the skeleton of a cholla, a rodent skull with four teeth missing, an old cow bone, a deer antler, a moth-eaten, ragged pine cone washed down from the mountains, and a bunch of hawk feathers tied up with a string.

There, in those drawers, the whole gamut of life, struggle, and death on the desert is revealed. How matter-of-factly the boys accept the reality that everything is both a hunter and is hunted, eats as well as is eaten—and I remember Kipling's "Law of the Jungle, as old and true as the sky." To fill a child with false sentimentality about the world of nature is doing him a disfavor when the truth of it is more comprehensible and the mystery acceptable. The boys' phrase, "That's the way things are," may not be as poetic as that of Kipling, yet it serves, usually. "But, Mother, why do coyotes eat rabbits and horses don't?"

Our stream in winter

2

The Stream

THOUGH my husband is now a museum director, he was first a herpetologist. This means that whenever possible he gives chase to snakes, lizards, frogs, toads, turtles, salamanders, and if they happen to be about, crocodiles and alligators, with the hardly believable intention of capturing them. This is a common boyhood disease that, far from outgrowing, Bill enlarged upon and embellished.

Herpetology is nurtured by, and in some cases is dependent upon, one of the most persistent, yet little known and recognized, drives in man, namely that of the collector. Often it will outshine such lesser urges as the desire for food or shelter. The collector is born, not made, but fortunately the genes carrying this formidable impulse are confined to few of the higher mammals and are almost nonexistent in the lower echelons with the notable exception, some may say, of the pack rat. The collector indefatigably collects from the moment his fingers can first close around a foreign object until the greatest collector of them all permanently removes him from this earth. And the crux of the matter, as far as the collector is concerned, is not *what* he collects, but that he *must* collect.

Collections are unconfinable. The bureau drawer overflows to the bookshelves and from there to the closet and immovable boxes under the bed. Then the family, in desperation and if it can, provides a separate room where the collection can be housed in more or less dignity and splendor. The door is emphatically closed, everyone sighs, and there it will surely live happily ever after. But before the dust has settled, it is moving restlessly and relentlessly, and then slyly and stealthily it sneaks under the door and out.

So far our sons have not yet exhibited the single-minded dedication and tenacity of the true collector. They accumulate, with typical boyish enthusiasm, stamps, coins, Indian relics, fossils, sea shells, weapons, baseball cards, and marbles. I remember a remark Peter made when he was five: "I'm going to collect nothing but marbles and money!" But it went no further than this male boast cast upon the wind like the bark of a wolf cub. My husband is a different matter. He collected golf tees at the age of three with the same perseverance that he collected snakes at the age of twelve and Japanese invasion money during the war.

The world being what it is, for the collector simply to collect is not sufficient. A fundamental *raison d'être* is obligatory and so science enters the door. This remarkable branch of study can find a reason for almost anything, even for the amassing of snakes.

In zoological studies, I was told, many hundreds of flies or birds or moths—or whatever—must be collected, because it is only by the very careful study of the many that an accurate picture or description of the species can be constructed. It takes many snakes of exactly the same kind to delineate a general pattern into which they all must fit. After these patterns have been assembled, the species or race is known—until a new kind is found, or an old one found in a new place, and so on. This applies in studying all living things, from the gnat to the mountain lion. That is one scientific reason for collecting. There are others. But it all comes down to knowledge and understanding.

"For science" is so venerable a phrase, so loaded with dignity and importance, that it will affect even a young romantic female who has courtship on her mind. I spent my twentieth summer taking lizards' temperatures in the company of a young Tucson herpetologist who was accumulating data for the American Museum of Natural History. Whenever I mentioned my summer's occupation outside of the family, I was viewed with astonishment and morbid curiosity. But it did not seem in the least strange to me, so persuasive is science and a young scientist.

And it was during that rosy twentieth summer that I held my first snake. It was one of the two eight-foot Indian pythons Bill had brought back with him from the war. It hung over my arm, its tail dragging behind me in the dust and its head, with the dozens of teeth, held a few inches above the ground where it swayed gently to and fro close to my ankle. In frozen fear I watched the flickering tongue explore the air around my bare foot. It must have been at that moment that Bill decided that I would do. I never again wish to experience that feat, but not for a second do I regret its outcome.

The full realization of what is a herpetologist has come to me gradually over the years. To others it usually comes far more explosively. It came to an uncle of mine when he arrived at La Guardia Airport to see off his younger son who was making his first trip west in our company and that of a boa constrictor. It came to an uncle of my husband when he accidentally swallowed a baby horned toad that was spending the night at the bottom of a glass by his bedside. Moments later when the reptile reappeared, Bill was there to catch it. "Oh, good, Unc!" said the boy, "you didn't hurt the horned toad at all!" And it came to a friend when, for five exciting minutes, he watched Bill thrash about in the middle of the Pacific, futilely trying to catch a highly venomous sea snake with a butterfly net. "So that," sighed our friend, "is a herpetologist."

It is in the happy hunting grounds of Arizona, blessed with having seventeen different kinds of rattlesnakes alone, that a herpetologist really flourishes. So, after my husband completed his graduate studies at the University of California in Berkeley, we packed up our belongings, our two sons, our dog, and the numerous bottles of pickled specimens and hurried back to the desert. There Bill became Zoologist for the Arizona-Sonora Desert Museum which was just opening its doors outside of Tucson.

As zoology includes all fauna, his field of interest necessarily expanded, and inevitably conservation has become one of his chief concerns. His desire for precise knowledge includes not only an awareness of the beauty of the natural world and the joy to be derived from merely looking at it, but also a gleeful appreciation of man's precarious place as the present dominant life form on an insignificant planet. Since life, the experiment of which man is but one example, has as much of a future as it has a past, I'm sure he's quite convinced that, given the necessary time, busy nature will evolve something far more important and interesting than man, or perhaps that is his hope.

Before long my husband was well settled in his new job and we were settling down in our new house in a portion of our own desert. Slowly we became familiar not only with what was outside our door but with the adjacent stream. To me, a riparian, the stream is a welcome contrast to the desert. It is much that the desert is not. It is soft and green and damp, with shady trees and bushes and flowers. Here the seasons wheel by with their traditionally visible changes, and the eye is charmed by less frugal fare. It is a more immediate, affable, and accessible world, and though it undoubtedly will not develop the strong self-reliant character in one that the desert will, it is so very agreeable. I can sit on the bank, wrapped in a cocoon of idleness, and delight in the loveliness that is all around thoroughly and unabashedly. Not once have I been moved, like poor Petrarch, to take a copy of St. Augustine's *Confessions* from my pocket, "Angry with myself that I still admired earthly things." Here life is not just a means to an end, nor is it a bounden duty; it is enough that one should admire and enjoy it, and yes, be thankful when the stream is running.

Sadly, it does not run all year, but only during the months of the summer and winter rains. In the days before over-grazing and over-pumping had lowered the underground water table, our stream did run all year and our rivers contained at least some water. Early residents spoke of beaver dams, of duck hunting in the marshes along the Santa Cruz that bordered Tucson's west side, and of the prevalence of malaria. The July 17, 1887, newspaper reported the catching of a nine-pound fish in that same river, the Santa Cruz, and an army officer, on being transferred from Tucson out to Fort Lowell (now part of the city), was reported to have been delighted to have moved to where the fishing was even better.

Heavy grazing, before the turn of the century, destroyed much of the protective plant-cover, so that runoff after rains greatly increased, causing erosion and the cutting of channels. Our once grassy water courses changed considerably in character and are now eroded, steep-banked, sandy river beds that are dry except when a cloudburst fills them for a few hours with muddy water.

In no time at all we wore a path from the house down to where, close by the stream, a large sycamore tree grows, spreading out its white-barked branches over a flat sandy space. On one side, between a mesquite and a catclaw, we strung a hammock, and on

John crossing the stream

John and bobcat

the other side we gathered a few rocks to support a grill. This
outdoor living room is a practical and constantly used extension
of the house, which has the added advantage of never needing to
be vacuumed.

Along this path we pass and repass, one procession blending
into the next; and under the trees we find the shadows of our
former selves. As I walk along through the purple asters and yellow
daisies, I look back to another October. First I see the bounding
dog. Next comes Peter followed closely by John, both barefoot, in
red bathing suits, carrying toy sailboats, and discussing the dead
dove by the side of the path, badly shot by some hunter. "What a

From left to right: Peter, John, Hugh, and Michael (fall, 1958)

dreadful life they lead," says John. "I wouldn't want to be a dove."

After a short gap comes Hugh, naked, fanny wagging as he walks cautiously so that he won't step on a burr. He carries two shovels in one hand and a pail in the other. Mike, also naked, follows Hugh, pulling a wagon in which he has put his stuffed rabbit, a dump truck, and a small garden hoe. He keeps shouting to Hugh. "Hugh . . . hurry. Hurry, Hugh!" Our bobcat stalks the rabbit in the wagon. He leaps out from behind a bush and with his paw swipes at the rabbit, which is on the verge of falling out. His last charge is successful, the rabbit is on the ground, and he is about to seize it and run off with it when Mike turns around and rushes to his rabbit's rescue. This time he tucks it under his arm and the procession resumes.

Each child carefully steps over a fifty-cent-piece hole in the middle of the path. It is a tarantula's hole and Hugh pauses to peer into it, hoping to see the owner, a female who has been living there several years; but only after a summer rain do we sometimes see a few long hairy legs protruding from it. Being a traditionalist, she sticks close to home, leaving the wandering to the males.

On reaching the stream we scatter. The dog goes off on a private chase. Michael and Hugh establish themselves in the sand. Peter and John head for the biggest pool to sail their boats. But first they catch a few caterpillars, which they install as crew, though in moments of generosity they allow them to be passengers so as "to enjoy the view"! They do not pick up the bristly-gray buckmoth caterpillar whose stinging hairs leave painful welts.

The bobcat goes with them. He walks gingerly from rock to rock, lifting each paw as it gets wet and shaking it. His progress is slow and halting, but at last he arrives at the small island and

Our bobcat Tamberlane

sits watching the boats sail by. When one comes close, he approaches longingly to the water's edge. Soon the enticement of such a prey is too great, and he plunges into the water and swims rapidly after the boat, only his head and the tip of his short tail visible above the water. He overtakes the boat, but after a sniff or two decides that it is not as interesting as he had thought and so swims back to the bank, climbs out, shakes himself, and goes to where the two younger boys are making roads and digging in the sand. He jumps on top of a newly completed castle, expertly flattening it. He knocks down a bridge, leaves large paw marks all over the smooth roads, and then tries to fit himself into Hugh's hole. These activities infuriate the boys, who yell at him to go away, right now, and leave them alone, they're busy! Discouraged, he comes to join me and lies down to wash himself, or is it to dry himself? He stays there until, out of the corner of an eye, he catches sight of John climbing a tree, and he runs off to join him up in the branches.

 I am sprawled on the golden bank of the afternoon watching

Peter and Tamberlane

the large cool shadows eat up the bright splashes of sunshine on the grass. Overhead yellowing leaves of the sycamore are rustling gently against the sparkling sky. A small white cloud, the only one about, is snagged on the farthest branch, and high, where the air is thin, a silent silver plane is dividing the sky with its glistening vapor trails.

The sense of coming winter is all around. The air is filled with the nutty smell of things drying and dying, and the water just beyond my head is carrying fall's first leaf-boats over the reflections. In a few weeks the sycamore leaves will have turned to copper and those of the cottonwoods, ash, and willows to gold. They will spread their images in profusion over every smooth stretch of water, thus dazzling the passerby with a double magnificence. Standing out brilliantly against the monochromatic desert, they can be seen from afar, outlining the course of the stream, which has metamorphosed into a river of fire. Here visible fall is as exuberant and colorful as anywhere else, but it is confined to the larger washes and river beds where the water is closer to the surface and the larger-leafed trees can therefore grow.

And as I listen to the sound of flowing water I think of our stream's long journey that begins in the pine forests which trim the top of the Catalina Mountains like a toupee. I wonder at its mysterious birth six thousand feet above us. Does it suddenly bubble out from under a rock, a thin silvery trickle at once as fragile and as tenacious as any newborn; and as it goes, grow like all living things, gathering momentum? Squirrels, swaying in the evergreen branches, must watch it, and screeching jays fly over it. In the spring, violets and columbine nod beside it, and in the winter, snow and ice smother it into silence and immobility. Down it comes through a deepening gorge, through piñon and pine, through scrub oak and manzanita, winding nearly twenty miles in and out of the slowly changing and dwindling vegetation, down to the hot, arid desert. Deer drink from it as it passes, as do the coons, porcupines, and bobcats. Even so will the bear and mountain lion.

What an incredible voyage it is, for in its six-thousand-foot descent this stream of ours passes through as many changes in vegetation as it would if it started thousands of miles away in northern Canada. Before it leaves the mountains, great canyon walls tower above it, as up above had towered the pines. At last it wanders out through the foothills to us. All it ever brings from the place of its birth is an occasional waterlogged pine cone, but that is enough to remind us of its travels.

Walking back to the house the long way, up the stream, past the small beach to where the wash comes in, and then up it to the path leading back to the house, we pause briefly at the beach to look for animal tracks along the water's edge. Sure enough, we see where a coon has come to drink and to fish for tadpoles. Several times we have found deer tracks and once the large pad-marks of a mountain lion. Then, in a moment of anxiety, I asked my husband what would happen if a boy, a nice chubby little boy, were to wander past a bush behind which a mountain lion was resting. "Would he attack?" "Not out of meanness!" was his reply.

As we walk along I comment on the two dead willows collapsing on the opposite bank and suggest that we should have them chopped up into firewood. "Oh, no!" says Hugh, true son of his father. "We're lucky to have them. That's part of our beauty." Nature, I find, can sometimes do with a little straightening. "Not so!" say the male members of the family and I am outnumbered.

The boys collect seeds as they go, first the hard round sycamore balls that hang in clusters of two or three, then the milkweed pods and the lovely delicate Chinese-like lanterns of the groundcherry. The milkweed pods they open and set the filamentous parachutes adrift on the afternoon breeze. But the prize is always a devils-claw, and envied is he who discovers a vine scattered with these pods which, when split open and dried, look like small ice-tongs. The remainder of the walk will then be spent in the elaborate machinations of trade. Not until I became the mother of four sons did I fully appreciate the inventiveness and persistence of the bargaining male. When the haggling reaches its peak, I might well be in the middle of an Arab market; the boys are less romantic perhaps, but just as noisy.

As ingenious as one brother may be in extricating a devils-claw from another, they are amateurs compared to the ingenious-ness of nature in insuring that its desert flora will reproduce successfully. Not only is the usual infinite variety in the manner in which seeds scatter themselves employed, but the hardiness of the seeds themselves is little less than phenomenal. Such a fragile plant as the evening primrose will produce seeds that can lie dor-mant in the dust for years until the suitable conditions of rain and warmth revive them.

Around the house, which lies on the borderline between the desert and the bottomland, autumn is also leaving its signs, though less obviously. The harvester ant is busily stripping my pyracantha bushes of their tenderest leaves. These he carries down into his nest deep underground to make into a mulch for fertilizing the fungus he grows for food. Under the lantana shrubs the ground is covered with butterfly wings, and the butterflies that still hover among the fading blossoms look frayed and sad. Our leaves, however, have not yet begun to turn, because the few feet that we are above the stream is enough to make a marked difference in the temperature. Were we to live in the foothills themselves the temperature change would be even more dramatic, a twenty-degree difference sometimes existing between the stream's edge and a hilltop.

Along our south fence the buzzards are beginning to congre-gate in preparation for their flight south. In the early morning we count dozens of them roosting in the trees and bushes, on top of the telephone poles and fence posts, some spreading their wings to the warming sun. Once, during this time of year, I fell asleep on a sand bar in our stream with the water lapping at my feet, and when I awoke, twenty-three buzzards were circling me, close enough so that I could see their naked red heads wagging as their greedy eyes inspected me. I suppose they were trying to decide who would get what. Half asleep, I saw myself as they saw me, and to those wheeling birds I was merely dinner, skimpier than a cow but happily bulkier than a rabbit. And I could see my tomorrow's bones scattered among the claw prints in the damp sand.

Having been momentarily leveled to a buzzard's dinner must have left an unsuspected mark upon my subconscious, for several nights later I dreamed that a thick black column of buzzards was flying directly over our house headed south. Then, in my dream, I saw the buzzards that roosted in our trees fly up into the air to join the others. And the next morning not a single buzzard was left; they had actually gone. So I became psychic to buzzards—alas, an unproductive faculty.

And out on the desert the year proceeds as usual with no sign of the slowly approaching winter.

*　　*　　*

Now it is winter. Two frosts and a heavy-handed wind have stripped the trees of leaves. It is early morning and a mist still lies thick in the valley. Along the stream the spider webs have gathered their nightly quota of liquid beads, which at last give them substance, and again I am surprised at how many of them there are. The black, bare-branched trees are spectral, a confusion of spidery lines that some mysterious nighttime creature has traced on the clouded sky.

On a branch a phoebe sits, its feathers still ruffled against the cold. Under a bush a towhee scratches in the moist earth, and a warbler hops about in a hackberry tree, waiting for the mist to lift and the bugs to fly again. Though it is winter the most hardy of the insects are alive and active, the frosts not being intense enough to kill them. With a year-round supply of bugs and seeds assured, many of our birds are permanent residents except most notably the buzzards, the white-winged doves, the nighthawks, and the kingbirds; and also a number of winter visitors are attracted, such as the ruby-crowned kinglet, the water pipit, and the Audubon's warbler.

The mountains, which always orient one, today are covered with clouds, and so, in this small valley, one loses all sense of where one is. The clouds do not lift, but spread out to cover the sky, and by late afternoon a few flakes of snow are squeezed out of them. If we are lucky we may have a brief snow flurry of large wet flakes that melt soon after landing. But every few years the snow will actually cover the ground for a day or two and then the schools declare a holiday. I remember once, when the boys were gathered in front of a window watching the miraculous performance of snow falling, I overheard Peter explaining the phenomenon to his brothers: "It's snow. Daddy says it is."

Down by the stream the white mantle, though unaccustomed, is worn naturally, but the sight of a cactus capped with snow is outlandish. Our dog will go wild with excitement and rush around in a frenzy only slightly more exuberant than that of the boys. And the rabbits and ground squirrels hop about this new white world with cold feet and perplexity.

However, the fingers of winter usually touch lightly here, though the rain to us can seem very cold, so cold in fact that Hugh once remarked that God must have put ice cubes in the watering can. And signs of winter more common than snow are evident. The reptiles are hibernating; no longer do lizards scuttle out from under the bushes as we pass. Only the gray tree lizards, whose small bodies respond quickly to the sun's heat, may be seen on a warm day clinging to the bark of a tree, and the brownish side-blotched lizards, almost invisible as they bask in the sun-warmed sand close to a bush. In January the fuzzy buckmoths dot the screen doors. And winter is a good time to collect praying mantis egg cases. These hard, golden-brown lumps, the size of a nickel, are glued to a twig, and when the trees have shed their leaves, are easily visible.

Winter is brief, with spring lurking behind the skirts of February, ready to pounce. From the top of a saguaro a thrasher begins to sing wildly and joyously, exhorting the world to burgeon. He fashions a golden snare of sound with notes as varied and mellifluous as those of his cousin the mockingbird, and the heart of the listener is swept up into the luminous air where it trips lightly from note to note mesmerized by a moment that seems eternal. At last, when released by silence, it returns, glowing with jeweled dust, and I am grateful to the thrasher for having shared with me his ecstasy of the sunlight and the coming spring.

Down by the stream everything is still hushed and waiting. February is clothed with a wonderful somnolence heightened by the soft calls of the mourning dove, by the softening air, by the warm pale sunlight. Even the stream is quiet, its reflections mere impressionistic suggestions of the resting world around. Occasionally a fitful breeze will slip off the newly powdered mountain tops to bring a faint frostiness by way of reminder that elsewhere things are different.

Then comes spring with its darting eyes, and we are caught up in the frenetic Priapic burst of activity. If during the two or three months after Christmas we have our expected rainfall, or a bit more, the lavishness, the profusion, the very miracle of spring will leave us breathless. The Easterners here for the first time think us mad, for we talk of nothing else but of the green and the flowers, common fare where they come from. The desert is not a desert when it has rained. It is almost a meadow. Everything is swathed in green and hardly a prickle shows. We are so unused to wild flowers that when they start popping out of the ground I find myself telling the boys to watch where they walk, as if I had planted and cared for each one.

"When is the desert in bloom?" is a question often asked of my husband. It is unanswerable because different plants bloom at different times. A few days after a dinner party during which this situation was discussed by some Philadelphia friends of ours, we received a postcard from Tombstone depicting Boot Hill cemetery where the graves of the desperadoes were decorated with artificial flowers. "At last," wrote our Philadelphia friends, "we have seen the desert in bloom."

In the spring, say late February on into April, providing

Evening primroses in March

the preceding months have been rainy, the desert will be carpeted with wild flowers, the small, yellow, delicate bladder-pod appearing first, followed by lupine, gold-poppies, desert-marigold, paperflowers, and desert verbena. The cacti, however, don't reach their peak until late April or May. Then it is that the small, compact, perennial shrubs like the zinnia and the brittle-bush are covered with white or yellow blossoms and that the palo verde seem dipped in sunshine, turning the foothills to billowing gold. The catclaw

hides its thorns behind fuzzy caterpillar blooms, and the desert-willow is covered with fragile, pale-lavender trumpet flowers.

Often, on a spring afternoon, I lie under a mesquite tree and listen to the stream, which runs deep and clear. The banks are covered with grass and clover, and where I have matted it down the hot sun draws out the moist sweet smell of things growing. Flowers are scattered everywhere. Close to the water monkey-flower grows, elsewhere lavender owl-clover and phacelia, clumps of poppies like Easter eggs, yellow mustard, and borage. Every insignificant weed is wearing some tiny blue, purple, yellow, or white jewel that reveals its beauty only on close inspection. Great mops of deer grass line the banks with drooping tips that sweep the ground whenever the wind blows. And in the water itself is a patch of pepperwort, a very primitive fern with leaves like a four-leaf clover that causes a pollen expert's eyes to light up.

I hear the chirp of a black phoebe and I watch it dart about. It is joined by its mate and together they sit in a tree, while below them an exceedingly fat robin investigates the bank and then hops down to the water for a drink. A group of noisy house finches fly by like a gang of giddy girls just let out of school. Very high in the clear air two ravens soar and tumble in ecstatic acrobatics, tracing on the sky an infinite variety of baroque curlicues. Spring has enchanted them, for never have I seen ravens fly so nimbly and with such grace.

I am not an ardent birdwatcher. I like to wait under a tree and let the birds come to me if they so desire, though I have been on bird walks with ornithologists. These I find frustrating, the bird always having flown before I see it. Ornithologists claim to have seen as many as sixty-three species of birds along our stream, a fact I feel no compulsion to prove but of which I boast. They tell me that we live in a particularly fortuitous spot because we not only have the desert birds but also some of the mountain ones, such as the white-breasted nuthatch and the scrub jay, that drift down the canyon in the stream of cold air. We even have nesting pairs of the rare rufous-winged sparrows, and occasionally a pair of ducks will stop in, or a blue heron, or an egret.

On the other side of the stream a Gila woodpecker scolds the dog, who is sniffing at a rock squirrel hiding beneath his tree, and a pair of vermillion flycatchers are briskly chasing flies. It is easy to follow the brilliant red male, less easy to see his drab-brown mate. When a Cooper's hawk flies by, dipping in and out of the trees, everything is suddenly silenced. Nothing moves, nothing sings. Everything waits, as if some mysterious hand has pulled a switch and all life is instantly frozen. The hawk disappears upstream. Seconds go by and then a sparrow begins to sing, tentatively at first until others shake themselves and catch up the song. The shadow of danger is dissolved by splendid sound, and spring goes pulsing on more jubilantly than ever.

If I had my way, I would shoot that Cooper's hawk. I resent his filling his belly with our pretty songbirds. The stream appears to be a trap, luring small birds to it with the promise of food and water, and then loosening on them their mortal enemy. Should I mention my murderous intentions to my husband, he would only look at me with shock and chagrin, for obviously I have not grasped the fundamental law of nature, that one species has as much right to live and eat as another, and that the songbirds are as much the hawk's to eat as they are mine to listen to.

I watch a handsome black-and-orange swallowtail butterfly flit by, the sun shining through its wings; and close at hand with a Gulliver eye I watch a ladybug struggle up the stalk of a fiddleneck, a spotless ladybug. On the next stem a gaudy blister beetle sets out for a dinner of leaves. This beautiful creature secretes an irritating fluid that discourages small boys, as well as those who might wish to make a meal of him, from picking him up. I think, as I lie there, that the real luxury of time is not merely to have enough of it in which to get done all the things that one wishes, but to have enough to squander idly, in clover, like this.

Back a ways from the stream, under the mesquite, the ground is white with evening primroses. Our first spring here my husband walked down to the stream one evening and in the dusk saw white splotches everywhere. He naturally concluded that some ill-behaved child had tossed Kleenex about and began to work up a fury, but as he reached down to pick up the nearest piece he found, instead, a flower. So, for a few weeks, our world is strewn with spires, sprigs, plumes, pompons, wisps, and froth; and through it all I sneeze and scratch with hay fever.

Road-runner on nest in a cholla cactus

In April the mesquite fling wide their branches and are covered with new downy leaves. They, along with the catclaw, are the last of the trees to succumb to the sweet disorder of spring—no elegant *quattrocento* spring as Botticelli painted it, but an urgent one, which knows its time is brief.

Everywhere birds are building nests, sitting on eggs, or feeding voracious young. The boys and I take a nest-viewing tour. First we stop to see the road-runner that sits determinedly on a large sprawling nest in the middle of a cholla. All that we can see of her is her long tail sticking up amidst the spines. She spaces her eggs as does any intelligent modern parent; the first-born, being the largest, receives the most food, which gives him an advantage and increases the possibility of at least one surviving. The road-runner is one of our favorite birds. No one can resist him, and he has rightly earned the nickname "the clown of the desert"—not surprising for a member of the cuckoo family. Once a road-runner found himself in the boys' play-yard and went running frantically around and around looking for a way out, forgetting that he was first and foremost a bird and could therefore easily fly over the fence.

In another cholla nearby a thrasher has laid three beautiful eggs, pale bluish with brown freckles, and next door a house finch is sitting on two clear-blue ones. This clump of cholla is a veritable bird maternity ward. Certainly, if one does not mind the spines oneself, the cholla provides excellent protection.

The mesquite thicket along the stream is another favorite nesting place. On one side of the path a canyon towhee has produced four white eggs splotched with purple in a neat nest of woven grass. On the other side a pair of Abert's towhees are already feeding their young. The tiny cuplike nest of a black-chinned hummingbird clings to a branch of a small ash next to the water, and in the large sycamore baby hooded orioles swing in their suspended home.

The younger boys want to see what has happened to a quail nest holding twenty eggs, so we walk up the wash to where the nest is lying on the ground near a pack rat's home. The nest is empty except for a few broken shells. Hugh picks up the eggshells and says, "Oh, dear, that quail is a careless mother. She ought to build her nest in a cactus like the other birds."

Then Peter insists that we go to see the dove nest he discovered in the staghorn near the cattleguard. I am exhausted by the surrounding display of seething motherhood, and at the end of the day I am grateful that I am not a bird.

But sometimes I wish I were a twelve-year-old boy. In the sycamore close by our south fence we have built a tree house. It is large and sturdy, accommodating four boys in sleeping bags. The boys, mostly in the spring, take turns sleeping there with their friends. Up at the house, in my bed, I think of them enviously. I think of the primroses shining white in the moonlight, of the water over the rocks, of the round eye of the moon in a pool, of the call of an owl, of the warm breeze off the desert, which passes the house and me to bring to those sleeping boys the smell of honeysuckle. It must be good to be a boy in the spring in a tree house.

John and Tallulah, a young great horned owl

3

House Guests

"I LIKE your friend, he's got pets!" said Michael one day to his oldest brother. This criterion of popularity is indicative of the state of things at our house. Let's say you are the Fuller Brush man giving his yearly push to our doorbell. The door is opened by a small boy eating a popsicle and you are invited in to wait while he goes to find his mother. As this may take some time, you stand in the kitchen looking out into what is called the "living" part of the house.

The noise is deafening. A parrot is trying to outshriek the Three Stooges, who are bellowing to each other on the TV screen. The two boys watching the Three Stooges turn around periodically to shout at the parrot to shut up. This progression of sound spirals ever upwards. Between the two boys lies a German shepherd, scratching fleas. Cutting through the noise comes a woman's drill-sergeant voice: "PUT THAT DOG OUT!" On a couch in one corner a bobcat and a domestic cat sleep side by side in a patch of afternoon sun, oblivious to everything but their respective dreams. And on the buffet a large black tarantula in a glass cage tries to push up the lid with his front legs.

Only someone with the fortitude of a Fuller Brush man will stand his ground in the face of this onslaught of sound. I do not know which will surprise him most, that we will buy brushes or that he will escape undamaged by beak, tooth, or claw. Or maybe it's a question of innocence. Once a salesman patted our young coyote, muttering "good doggie"; another time an insurance agent sat on our sofa, stroking our sleeping bobcat with "nice kitty"!

The inanimate objects that the boys bring in from the desert and keep in their rooms may cause problems and minor irritations, but it is the animate ones, euphemistically called pets by the boys, that keep our private world spinning in its inherent fashion. This can be reduced to simple mathematics in which the ratio of "complications" to "pets" is somewhere in the neighborhood of five to one.

To begin with birds, our smallest pet was Peter's western kingbird. It had been orphaned while still a fledgling, was turned over to the Museum by the game department, and Peter offered to raise it. He kept it in a box in his room and fed it tiny pieces of hamburger. To give it an airing and let it see something of the world, Peter would carry the bird around on his shoulder where it would nestle up close to his neck. Being a meticulous child, he would first cover his shoulder with a diaper, as one might to burp a baby, and on this he placed his bird. This system kept the droppings off of his clothes, but our housekeeper was heard to remark, "Never thought I'd be washing diapers for a bird!"

Inside and out Peter walked around with his pet on his shoulder. With small bright eyes, it peered serenely at the passing scene, quite unaware that this was not the natural order of things in the bird world. Peter called it Margalo after a bird-character in a book I once read him but which neither of us now remembers. His Margalo was a very natty creature in pale gray with a black tail, a yellowish breast, and the typical flycatcher suggestion of a ruffled crown. The idyll of bird and boy lasted for several weeks and then Peter went off to California to visit his grandmother, leaving Margalo and a long list of instructions behind.

I moved the bird to our bathroom where it perched on the shower-curtain rod, dropping droppings into the tub if its tail were in the right direction, and waited for me to appear with the food. I discovered that a bird has two very busy ends. Feeding a young bird is a time-consuming proposition that will soon convince one that something is wrong with the old saw, "eats like a bird." A bird, or at least this one, eats like Henry VIII, and I was continually mystified as to why it did not explode. But after each meal it gulped, closed its eyes for a moment, and then opened them and eagerly waited for me to bring on more food.

The first day Margalo gave me to understand that it no longer liked hamburger by dropping the meat on the floor and continuing to cheep hungrily, so I called the University and was told that grasshoppers and crickets would do nicely. That afternoon I set off for the stream armed with confidence, a tea strainer, and a jar. After a half-hour of leaping about after grasshoppers I sat under a tree and wondered just how it was that I had arrived in life at the exhausting position of bird-feeder. As with most things, mine was a long and confused road, an imperceptible slipping into something from which I would have run had it suddenly presented itself before me. Life is dotted with sly events that with guileless smiles lead us farther along an unplotted pathway until we have passed the point of no return. So there I was, trying to cram one more grasshopper into a jar that already contained sixteen others bouncing about like jumping beans.

And that was only the beginning. The first time I presented a grasshopper to Margalo, the bird let go of it and I had to chase it all over the bathroom. Then I remembered reading that you can cause a young bird to open its mouth by passing a hand over its head, making a shadow such as a mother bird might make. This triggers a reflex as definite as that of hitting a human knee with a rubber hammer, and the bird's mouth pops open. It worked and with eyebrow tweezers I stuffed the grasshopper down into the bird's throat. With a large gulp it disappeared. Sometimes, though, Margalo had trouble swallowing this meal and would partially spit out the grasshopper, hold it in its bill, tap it on the shower curtain rod to quiet it, and then reswallow it. After a week of this

Cloudcuckooland I decided that Margalo was ready for the Museum.

Our most ridiculous bird, or rather birds, were a pair of young great horned owls. When we received them they were already feathered and of a formidable size, but not yet independent. They ostensibly lived in the west patio, sitting on the wall or in the mulberry tree blinking their eyes and dozing. With their lids half-closed over huge, round, somewhat bulging eyes, they reminded me of a certain dramatic actress. Like Balinese dancers they moved their heads back and forth whenever I approached, perhaps as a warning not to come closer or in an effort to see better, and the whole effect was ludicrous. If John should discover one of them outside of the patio, he would grab it with both hands, holding its wings tight to its body, and rush with it held way out in front of him back to where it belonged. The owls did not care for this manner of transportation and protested with a violent clicking of their beaks. These are one of the largest of our American owls, with a wingspread of four to five feet, so one is moved to treat them cautiously. They are very handsome, with tufts of feathers like horns, as yet only beginning to show in our youngsters.

The brother of our owls lived at the Museum, where he was also allowed his freedom. He sat either above the fish tank, decorating the labels below with white streaks, or above the cage of baby quail, which he examined minutely and undoubtedly hopefully. One day he swooped down and grabbed a pacifier out of a visiting baby's hand, and this marked the end of his freedom. He went to reside in one of the aviaries.

Our owls, not content to remain in the west patio for long, began to wander farther afield. At mealtimes this was inconvenient, as I would appear with the plate of horsemeat and the long forceps only to discover that the birds had flown, and I would then have to walk around listening for their distinctive hunger cries. Often I found them perched high up in a mesquite tree, and not

Hugh feeding Tallulah

by any amount of waving their dinner above my head could I persuade them to fly down to a branch that I could reach. They were convinced that I was their mother and their mother could jolly well fly up to them. To a thirty-five-year-old female biped who had long ago given up tree-climbing, this situation posed some problems. I would fetch the stepladder, place it under an owl, climb up, and with the forceps stuff the horsemeat down its gullet. Thank heavens I was not expected to eat it first myself and then regurgitate it into their mouths, as I might have been expected to do had they been pelicans.

Jimmy and Diana the bobcat

Except for mealtimes the owls were no trouble. They were aloof, lethargic, and on the whole unobtrusive. Occasionally one would float out of a tree and land on the edge of the swimming pool to stare at Hugh drifting around in the water in his inner tube, or come flapping silently like a giant moth out of the night to sit on the wall beside a startled dinner guest. As time went on they became increasingly difficult to find for their meals, eventually drifting off altogether.

Our most mischievous bird was Jimmy. He was a raven. He began his career as someone's pet but was given to the Museum, where he lived in boisterous freedom until the complaints that he bullied the children could no longer be ignored. As a means of solving the problem Bill brought him home to bully our own children and so I armed the boys with sticks and instructed them on how to stave off a raven. Ravens are monstrous, have obdurate black eyes, Cyranoesque beaks, and are forever curious. They smugly trundle forth on an endless round of investigations comforted by the fact that it was only a *cat* that curiosity killed. Jimmy was Falstaffian—a ribald, raucous, impudent, rascally rogue. And if you were about to wring his neck he would look up at you full of candor and wistfulness, "Banish plump Jack, and banish all the world."

The relationship between a raven and his host, a term I am using strictly in the biological sense, is similar to that of most parasites to their source of nourishment. They take what they wish without even the pretense of gratitude until they decide that more is to be gained by moving on. Then they blithely cast off the host who by then is a good deal worse for wear if alive at all, and take up residence in greener pastures.

Life for Jimmy was much more than just a bowl of cherries. It was a series of wild devisings. A typical Jimmy day goes like this. It begins at dawn as he gallumps heavily over the roof in an effort to rouse some human attention. Seeing it is the rising hour of every indecent raven, (for no raven can conceivably be thought to be otherwise) surely everyone else must also be up and about. Besides he wants his breakfast. As this does not produce the slightest indication of human activity, he flies down and proceeds methodically from window ledge to window ledge, pecking vigorously on the glass. Anyone who has seen the size of a raven's beak will understand the alarming proportions of this enterprise. We still manage to ignore him by burying our heads under the covers and trying to think of something else, so he goes back to the roof and spends a pleasant half-hour rattling his tin plate above our housekeeper's room.

After a large meal of bread crusts and dog food he hops to the edge of the roof and peers down at the cat, who is for one last peaceful moment placidly eating his breakfast. This picture of feline bliss is irresistible, so down swoops Jimmy to tweak the cat's tail, which sends the poor animal scurrying. While the cat watches from under a chair, Jimmy disdainfully pecks at his food, scattering it around in the gravel. Now it is time for his workout with the dog. They chase each other lustily back and forth for an hour or so, at the end of which time Jimmy retires to the garage roof with just enough breath left to shout down insults.

When Michael (then four) appears in the play-yard Jimmy shifts his field of operations. He sits on the trellis above the sand-box and peers down between the slats while rotating his head this way and that in order to see what delectable toy the boy has in his hand that he could remove, and to check on the whereabouts of the German Shepherd. If the dog is too close he swoops down, wiggling his tail feathers saucily in front of her nose, and skims over the play-yard fence and down the driveway with the dog in hot pursuit. Then quickly he dashes back to the boy, snatches away the toy, and carries it to the roof.

Suddenly he hears a familiar sound coming from the kitchen door and he rightly guesses that our housekeeper is about to hang out the wash. He does not fly down and peck off her nose as does the less ingenious blackbird of the nursery rhyme; instead he sneaks up close and hides behind a bush, awaiting his chance, for he knows that she wields a mighty effective broom. The minute her back is turned he skips over to the clothes basket, grabs a diaper, and flies off, dragging this white flag gaily behind him. When the laundry is arranged and our housekeeper has once again returned to the kitchen, Jimmy tightropes along the clothesline, struggling to disengage the clothespins. When successful he gives a cry of triumph and dashes away with the clothespin, leaving behind him a wet garment heaped on the ground.

Now it is time for him to investigate the neighbors, the closest of whom lives about half a mile away. Much to Jimmy's satisfaction the neighbor is deathly afraid of him as is her yappy, woolly, white dog. Fifteen minutes after his departure the telephone rings. "That awful raven of yours won't let me or Toutou out of the house!" shouts our neighbor. "Please come and get him!" So I drive over, catch Jimmy in a fish net, put him in the garbage can I have brought for the purpose, and take him home. I leave him in the can for an hour to think upon his sins, during which time he taps loudly on the sides, jumps up and down in a rage, and busily thinks up new impieties. Upon his release he shakes his feathers, scolds me rudely, and flies off in a huff to tease the tortoise eating grass on the lawn. The tortoise is the only one that can get the best of Jimmy. He withdraws into his shell and leaves the bird hopping exasperatedly outside.

His afternoon activities consist of pulling the aluminum foil off the roof, of finding and tearing up paper into shreds with which to litter Bill's clean desert, of sitting on the window sills and streaking them with white, of frustrating our bobcat by yelling at her and capering around just out of pouncing range, which is a raven's way of thumbing his nose.

When we go down to the stream for a picnic, Jimmy goes with us. He joins the single file and waddles proudly along between Michael and Hugh. His eagerness to accompany us is not due to any Wordsworthian appreciation of the beauties of nature; what he is anticipating is a choice goodie or two from the picnic basket. Also, he just might be able to play an unexpected trick on a dog or a bobcat or a boy. Hope springs eternal even in a raven's breast.

For over two months we raised Jimmy and Jimmy razed us, until my housekeeper and I were dreaming of raven pie. I was recounting our life of persecution one evening to Roy Chapman Andrews and he countered with raven tales of his own. Apparently two ravens accompanied one of his Gobi expeditions, and when bored these birds would huddle on the top of a truck, plotting their next move. Their favorite sport was pulling the tails of the camels, which induced them to stampede. This managed to produce a satisfying amount of confusion, even for a raven, and delayed the proceedings by some hours. What eventually happened to the ravens Dr. Andrews never said. Similarly catastrophic was what happened to another friend of ours. His raven, during a large cocktail party, pulled out all the ignition keys of the guests' cars and dropped them in the driveway.

Gradually Jimmy began spending more and more time with his cousins, his aunts, and his uncles, who were living in a grove of sycamore trees on the other side of the stream, until finally he never bothered to return at all, not even for a handout. I guess he grew bored with us, and the pain of ennui outweighed the pleasure of having his meals served to him.

In the bird line Bill has not yet realized his most cherished ambition. He wants to train two buzzards to sit above the front door and welcome our guests with a silent stare. I have not tried to fathom this secret desire of his, believing it best to let sleeping birds lie.

Our toothiest pet was an alligator. He lived in the boys' bathtub for one day. I was not of the opinion that bathtubs make satisfactory receptacles for three feet of alligator, so I said he would have to be lodged elsewhere. "Oh, mother! You're so old-fashioned!" I persevered and finally Bill took him down to the stream on the theory that plenty of aquatic life was about for him to eat. Whether he included the boys in this category I did not ask. Privately I had my suspicions. The picture of an alligator and four boys splashing in the same bit of stream is not one to set a mother's heart at rest.

During that summer the stream filled up twice with flood waters, but each time it subsided I found fresh alligator tracks on the sand bar. This was an adhesive alligator and I wondered what it would take to dislodge it. The answer was time. By September I saw no more alligator tracks and life suddenly looked much

Michael and Legs the tarantula

rosier. Several weeks later I read an article in the newspaper about how a Tanque Verde Valley resident had found an alligator swimming in his pool. The speculations on how he got there were elaborate, involving his having escaped from a carnival, having crossed several mountain ranges, and heaven knows what all. Luckily no one considered the natural law of moving water and who might be living upstream. We kept a discreet silence.

"Bugs," a term I am using loosely, have never been one of my particular enthusiasms, but my tolerance for them has definitely broadened, and what once would have caused my eyes to roll slackly in my head now only causes them to blink. During my abecedarian years a five-year-old Peter once appeared in the kitchen. "Look what I caught!" he proudly announced, holding out a jar in which rested a full-grown tarantula.

"Why, Pete, it's a beauty!" I managed to exclaim, remembering my Spock. "How did you ever catch it?"

"Well," said Peter, "I spied him crawling by the gate and I went and got this jar and walked up to him and put the jar over him and turned it over and put on the lid."

"That is very clever of you and won't your father be pleased to have him for the Museum."

But Peter did not know how the story is supposed to end. "This is *my* tarantula," he said emphatically, "and I'm going to keep him. Daddy can catch his own!" And thus he eliminated Prokofieff's triumphal procession to the zoo with the strings and brasses sounding grandly.

Several times that exulting march has gone through my head, the last time a few days ago when Peter and a friend of his came striding through the desert one behind the other. They each carried the end of a pole in the middle of which hung a bucket. In the bucket was one dead and one live rattlesnake and the boy in the back held a stick with which to poke down the head of the live rattler should it appear. Following them came the other boys like a tail to a comet.

When I was putting the new tarantula owner to bed for his nap, he insisted that the jar with the tarantula inside be placed beside him because "he's so cute. Don't you just love him!" When I went to awaken him the jar was lidless. Fortunately the spider must also have been napping, for he was still inside. When I asked for an explanation of why he had removed the lid, the child's answer was that he wanted him to have plenty of fresh air! Then it was that I drew up a list of rules for the keeping of tarantulas.

This tarantula marked the beginning of a long series of these hairiest of pets. As a matter of fact, I have grown quite fond of them, and for our present one I built in the middle of his terrarium a small tarantula house of mud and stones around whose entrance the spider quickly spun a neat web, and now it pops in and out in a very satisfactory manner. We call all our tarantulas

"Legs." Our American tarantula is unrelated except in name to the European wolf spider, which is the true tarantula whose bite was supposed to cause tarantism, a kind of frenzy imitated in the tarantella dance. Our tarantulas have a poison, as have all spiders, in order to paralyze their prey, but contrary to popular belief, they cannot in any way be considered dangerous. In all the years that we have been handling them, not one has even shown an inclination to bite. We feed ours mostly meal worms with occasional treats of grasshoppers or crickets, though the latter John removes if he sees.

My husband once told me of a professor, an outstanding authority on these spiders, who gave female tarantulas as wedding presents. Irrespective of all their other charms they make the most practical pets imaginable. They not only are easy to care for (they have been known to go over two years without food), but females may live as long as twenty-five years and anyone can see what an advantage that is. Your tarantula will see you through all kinds of important occasions: births, graduations, promotions. Perhaps you could end by giving it as a wedding present to one of your very own children, and what could be more romantic than that.

Do not be alarmed should you suddenly see, in your tarantula's cage, two instead of one. The second tarantula will be your pet's discarded suit, for he sheds his "skin" much as does a snake. And in common with most spiders, tarantulas when they shed can replace a missing appendage, so you will never be embarrassed by an unsightly imbalance in your pet's appearance should he suffer some mishap and lose a leg. Shedding also allows the female to renew her virginity by replacing the sperm pockets, so the Goddess Hera, for all of her airs, had nothing on a tarantula.

I have less appreciation for other arthropods that sporadically reside with us. Centipedes, scorpions, solpugids, and millipedes all leave me on the offensive. The only possible advantage to having a millipede around is that in a conversational lull you can fill the gap with "Sure, I know what a millipede is; it's like a

A praying mantis laying eggs

centennial only it has more legs." About ants I feel much like the little boy who wrote:

Ants is to kinds, insects and lady uncles. Sometimes they crawl into the sugar bole, and sometimes they live in holes with their married sisters. That's all I know about ants.

A yearly event that predisposes me more kindly towards "bugs" is the hatching out of the praying mantises. Every winter the boys manage to find at least one mantis egg case which has not been parasitized, and we enshrine it in a jar usually kept by the telephone. Watching those minute creatures struggle out through the shell one after another and then go stalking off, each an exact replica of their, by comparison, gigantic parent, is always a thrill.

Once this event took place as I was listening to a verbose lady declaim on how, because of our interest in animals, we should join the American vegetarian movement aimed at eliminating meat from our diets. Quickly losing the sense of the discourse and enraptured with what was taking place before my eyes, I unconsciously gave voice to a number of appreciative sounds which the lady at the other end of the wire took for full agreement to what she was at the moment saying. With a few breathy thank-you's and "You'll be hearing from us shortly, my dear Mrs. Woodin," she hung up. My perplexity and anxiety were profound for I hadn't the vaguest idea what it was I had agreed to, and for all I knew, I would be expected to picket the White House, with some such motto as EAT BEETS KEEP TRIM. And to this day I still don't know.

Not all of our bugs are confined to jars or glass cages and this is a source of some worry on my part. My husband keeps what he calls a balanced state of things in his study. Scorpions, spiders, flies, and an occasional lizard live there in diminishing or augmenting numbers. When I give this room its bi-annual cleaning, I am instructed not to disturb the wolf spider's web, clotted with the remains of recent meals, that is spread along the top of the north window. And at least one boy's room also has in it a wolf spider. On the whole I am unaware of them, but sometimes at the edge of a crack I will see a leg or two, or perhaps the glint of one of their eight eyes.

Our slyest and most sinister guest was a three-inch catfish John caught in the stream. We called him Poison Zoomack after that slit-eyed, mustachioed, top-hatted, and cloaked character who slunk around in the funny papers doing wicked deeds. We first put him in the fishbowl where three lovely fantail goldfish swam proudly around displaying elegant tails that rippled like gossamer as they moved. Poison Zoomack, in the face of such beauty, skulked at the bottom, trying to hide his whiskers. By the next morning the tails of the goldfish had been reduced to a few short wisps, and like maidens who have lost their long locks, the fish drooped inconsolably. We isolated Poison Zoomack in a bowl of his own, where he lived for several years unrepentant and unredeemed, and unfortunately never growing large enough to be featured at the dinner table.

The Purple People Eater also came from the stream. He looked like a large caterpillar with all his legs at one end. His eating habits were not socially acceptable, and after finding two dead deflated tadpoles floating on the surface of the aquarium, we transferred him to separate quarters. He was some sort of larva which we kept in order to see what he would turn into, but he died before his transformation. We have never found another Purple People Eater.

The largest pet we ever had was a wolf. She came to us as a fuzzy, gray, gangling creature not much different from a German Shepherd puppy. She lived outside with the dogs and was by far the gentlest and shyest of them all. Whenever we appeared outside she would bound up to us, nip our ankles, and then flop about in typical puppy fashion. The only thing that reminded us of her origin was the way in which she ate her food; she quite literally "wolfed" it down so that it disappeared in a matter of seconds. She died before she was a year old so we had little opportunity until much later to acquaint ourselves with wolves.

This particular animal was a gray wolf from Canada. Arizona, in the early days, could boast of two different subspecies of the gray wolf of which now only the smaller southern form, the Mexican wolf, still occurs, though rarely, within its borders. Known locally by the Spanish name lobo, it is systematically hunted down whenever it shows its face, because of the stock-killing habits of an occasional individual—an example of a group paying the penalties for the unruly behavior of a few of its members. The same is true to a lesser degree of the coyote. He is still considered a pest by the chicken farmer and the sheepman, but most ranchers are now beginning to realize that coyotes are beneficial, keeping the rabbit and rodent population under control, and the wiser of them encourage the coyote rather than shoot him.

We had a coyote whom we called Sammy. He was born at the

Museum and came to live with us at about the age of three months. He was the most ingratiatingly destructive and the nimblest of our animals. He too lived outside with the dogs, considering himself to be one of them, though by neither appearance or behavior could he possibly be mistaken for them. He had an alert foxlike face, delicate legs, and an exuberant bouncy style. I saw no signs of the dogs objecting to Sammy's assumption of brotherhood, and they all milled about in happy comradery. Sammy went with us on our walks, trotting along, his lovely bush of a tail held low behind him in good coyote fashion. If Susie, our largest dog, should be blocking his path, instead of going around her he would duck under her. When we stopped to examine a hole or to look for garnets, Sammy also stopped and crowded up to poke his nose into whatever it was we were grouped around.

Sammy was very friendly. He would rush up to you to be petted, and when you reached down to pat him he would grovel in that peculiar jackal-like way with his head twisted up so that he was looking back over his shoulder, and then smile the fawning smile of an obsequious courtier. He also had a slobbery habit of

Michael and the wolf

mouthing one's arm or leg, not in any way to be taken as an overture to serious eating. It was his way of showing you that you and he were friends.

He liked to play tug-of-war and he would appear around the corner of the house, holding high, and tripping over, some improbable item he had discovered. If the item were suitable, such as an old rag, then we would grab hold of one end, and the game that so delighted him would begin. More than likely though, the item would be one of the boys' sweaters or coats and then the effort to retrieve the garment taxed our ingenuity as well as our endurance. The only successful way to achieve one's end was to go off as if one didn't care. Sammy would look at you disappearing into the house, in astonishment and disbelief, and after a few shakes of his head so as to display the garment more enticingly, he would drop it and go to find something else. Occasionally we allowed Sammy in the bedroom. He would leap onto the bed and prance around as if all the world loved a coyote.

Soon after his arrival my husband decided that the time had come when Sammy should learn to yap properly, for we didn't want him ridiculed by the wild coyotes of the neighborhood. Sammy caught on quickly and the two of them would sit side by side in the evening on the hillside, yapping in splendid chorus. No whiffenpoofer could have been more pleased with the results than they, and they paused periodically to admire the echoes of their song.

Contrary to the mournful western ballads, coyotes seldom howl; rather they emit variously pitched yaps and yips, so that a single coyote has the knack of sounding like several. They are especially vocal during bright moonlight nights, though sometimes we hear them in the late afternoon and early morning. Their shrill, excited clamor electrifyingly animates the desert, bringing indoors a sense of its tingling wildness. It is an eerie sound, which turns the night into a restless and precarious place and sharpens one's feeling of safety behind closed doors. I never hear them but that I picture in my mind a bushy, tawny form loping lightfootedly along.

When two English children and their nanny spent a few days in our guest house, they appeared for breakfast the first morning wide-eyed and shaken. During the night they had heard the coyotes yapping immoderately as they went about their business and had thought they were being surrounded by a pack of starving wolves. They did not need to be reminded what wolves did to the people they caught. To unaccustomed ears our ululating nighttime desert is alarming. The nanny not only locked the door but pushed the bureau in front of it to further reinforce it. Those English children provided a story telling challenge to our boys, and from the snatches of conversation I overheard, they must have departed with an astounding concept of our daily life.

The day Sammy discovered the cover to our swimming pool was sheer disaster. We keep a plastic cover over our filterless pool

Sammy ripping the pool cover

to prevent small children and leaves from falling in and to inhibit the growth of algae so that we do not have to clean it more than two or three times a year. The morning that Sammy experimentally stepped out onto the pool cover marked its end. First he spent some time dancing around in exuberant delight, grinning from ear to ear. The cover, resting on the surface of the water, perfectly supported his weight, and the strange sensation of walking on water he found to be enormously amusing. After experimenting with walking he tried running and then leaping. What a time he had! Then he made another discovery. He nipped a corner of the cover, and holding the material between his teeth, he began to pull. As he retreated backwards an increasingly long strip of plastic came with him. In a matter of hours he had reduced the cover to tatters and had littered the desert with countless pieces of plastic.

In the evening we often play badminton, a game Sammy thought was devised purely for his own pleasure. He would sit on the edge of the court waiting for someone to miss the bird. As soon as it touched the ground he was upon it; seizing it in his mouth, he would then dash off a ways and wait for us to chase him.

To our domestic cat Sammy paid not the slightest attention, and the bobcat in residence at that time was not allowed to venture outside, so the two could only gaze at each other curiously through a window or a screen door.

One day Sammy disappeared and he never came back to the house. We hoped that disaster had not overtaken him but that instead he merely had had a sudden urge to join his wild cousins who chattered nightly around the house. Sometimes when we see a coyote crossing our road we hopefully call out "Sammy, here Sammy!" but the animal pauses only briefly to survey us before trotting on. "I guess he has forgotten us," sadly explains Hugh.

One early morning a coyote tried to entice our German shepherd off into the desert and the boys were convinced it was Sammy come back for his old playmate. As the barking dog advanced, the coyote trotted slowly off, then sat down until the dog grew closer.

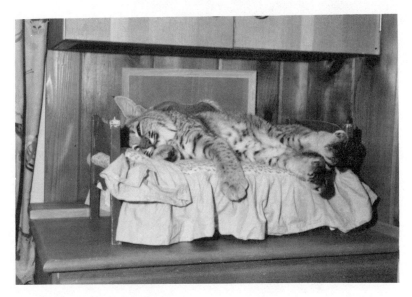

Penthesilia in the doll bed

Again he moved off and again waited for her to approach. Bill, who was less romantic, was of the opinion that this was an ill-intentioned coyote who might have had a few buddies hidden in the wash awaiting the arrival of the dog upon whom they would leap and then kill.

Animals arrive inside our house in all kinds of ways. Lizards and toads sneak in through cracks, snakes are carried in by the cat, butterflies fly in through open doors, birds fall down the chimney. They also arrive in snake bags or in the pockets of boys. Once during a dinner party my mother-in-law remarked to me, "What an adorable owl you have. I thought for the longest time that he was stuffed, but then he winked an eye. However did you train him to sit so quietly?" Knowing of no such creature in residence at the moment, yet prepared for anything, I looked in the direction in which she was staring, and sure enough, on top of the book-cases sat a screech owl gazing solemnly down upon the assem-

A visiting screech owl

bled company. All evening he sat there, immobile except for a periodic slight revolution of the head and a wink or two.

Another time the doorbell rang announcing the arrival of a dinner guest, and when Bill opened the door he noted on the ground beside the man a large tarantula also waiting to come in. "I didn't know you were bringing a friend," said Bill, "but we are glad to have both of you." The guest looked around in bewilderment, and just as the idea was forming that perhaps his host had double vision or worse, he caught sight of the tarantula near his foot and with a gasp and a leap he was inside the door. He was one of those who do not like spiders, least of all tarantulas.

One afternoon while I was rinsing my hair in the bathroom sink, I noticed two eyes looking into my upside-down ones. We stared at each other for a few seconds and then I withdrew my head. The owner of the other pair of eyes was a small treefrog who had found a suitably damp refuge in the overflow outlet under the front lip of the sink. Not long after, I came into our bedroom and discovered the bobcat's water dish completely filled with a large Colorado River toad who was dozing contentedly. He had accidentally made his way into the house and had spotted the only accessible bit of water.

Once I came into the living room to find John sitting in a chair with a full-grown cottontail cradled in his arms. The rabbit

Michael feeding a young jack rabbit

was lying on its back, glassy-eyed, with all four paws in the air. "I found him in the kitchen playing with Toby and Nandy (our cat and dog)," explained John. After much persuasion, for he wanted to keep the rabbit as a pet, John carried him to the woodpile and set him free beside a hole between the logs.

Every spring our pet population takes an upswing spurred on by the natural results of parturition. The Museum, in accord with the Arizona Game and Fish Department, strongly urges that baby animals be left in the wild, for a number of reasons. It is often against the law to collect them; the very immature have a poor chance of survival in captivity; and the wild baby that looks abandoned generally has a mother close at hand. Inevitably, however, spring brings its share of genuine orphans to the Museum, and although most of these are raised in the Museum nursery, there is always an overflow for which the boys volunteer as foster mothers.

Baby ground squirrels, baby birds, baby rabbits breathe softly in boy-made nests in small boxes. The boys respond to the vulnerability of these tiny creatures and faithfully feed them at regular and numerous intervals with medicine droppers full of milk. Sometimes the story ends successfully and the creature grows into a healthy adult and returns to the Museum; sometimes it ends sadly, the animal dies, and a new hole is dug in the cemetery under the mesquite trees. I can still remember the first of these occasions when John came to stand beside our bed early one morning, a dead ground squirrel in his hand. Mutely he held it out to us, tears welling out of his eyes and running down his face. He was crying for the small animal for which he had so lovingly cared, but I think he was also unconsciously crying for the very frailty of life itself. Children, with their outward-turning eyes, encompass more than we imagine.

And I shall never forget the anguished shrieks of everyone concerned when Penny the bobcat seized Peter's baby rabbit. I think the rabbit died of fright rather than of the injuries it sustained, but that mattered little in the face of its death. It was buried in a shoe box on which had been written in large black letters: PETER RABBIT'S—*MURDERED* BY PENNY THE BOBCAT.

Penny caused the untimely end of another resident, Alexander the parrot. Alex was bold and liked to spend his afternoons strutting on the kitchen counters. The first day after his arrival he had settled both the dog's and the domestic cat's hash by rushing at them with widespread wings and open beak, so they did no more than eye him from a safe distance. Confident of his supremacy, Alex paid no more attention to Penny than he did to the others as he swaggered arrogantly around the kitchen. Twenty-five hundred years ago *hubris* ended in tragedy, but Alex turned a lordly ear away from even ancient warnings. So one day Penny caught him and he now rests in the cemetery.

One particular spring a swarm of honey bees fastened themselves to the facing outside of my husband's study. The boys, no bee-masters, were stung so regularly that we had to exterminate the bees. I am not overly fond of bees, but I had thought it would be convenient to have our own honey manufactured on the premises. As it was, honey did run down our walls for several months afterwards. When a colony starts to become crowded, the workers, without the consent of their queen, begin to feed special food to several of the regular worker eggs and to enlarge their cells, thus stimulating the larvae to transform into queens. Then some of the bees swarm, taking the old queen with them. Last spring we found a mass of them, about the size of a football, clinging to a creosote branch. Periodically scouts flew off in search of a nesting place, and they must have been successful, for a few days later they were gone.

Then came the spring that Peter had a baby ground squirrel, John a baby pack rat, and Michael a spiny lizard with two tails, a not unusual occurrence in lizards. One of its defense mechanisms is a tail which breaks off readily and keeps on wriggling, thus distracting the enemy. The lizard then grows a new tail. Sometimes the tail is injured sufficiently to cause the growth of a new one without loss of the old, so that the lizard ends up with two tails.

That spring Hugh watched his brothers busily attending to their respective animals and walked around disconsolately carrying an empty shoe box in the hope of finding something to put into it that would become *his* pet. First he tried a wolf spider, next a caterpillar, and then three tadpoles in a jar of water. But none of these were at all satisfactory, for they either escaped or died, ". . . and besides," said Hugh, "you can't really hold those kinds of things and pet them." So once again he walked around with his empty shoe box, very much like A. A. Milne's little boy who took his penny to the market square because "I wanted a rabbit, a little brown rabbit, and I looked for a rabbit 'most everywhere."

Hugh did not find a rabbit though he looked under bushes and into holes, but he did find a small toad. It fit nicely into the palm of his hand, and best of all, it stayed there. To be sure, a toad is not exactly a rabbit, but to Hugh it was just right. "Aren't you a lucky woman," he said, full of satisfaction, "to have boys that can catch so many things."

John feeding Tiger Balm

4

Bobcats

OUR first fall in the desert had barely begun when Bill came home from the Museum with three baby bobcats. They were almost double ordinary kitten size, very fluffy, with short fuzzy exclamation-mark tails, ears ending in tiny black tufts, and tiger faces similar to those of the angelic kittens which used to appear in the Chesapeake and Ohio Railroad advertisements.

The care of bobcats, as with all young animals (including children) revolves around their stomachs. I approached the first meal confidently, the formula properly warmed in our youngest son's bottle. I took the precaution of wrapping up the infant in a diaper, which was relatively successful in keeping its sharp claws from imbedding themselves in my hands, but the nipple was too large and the kitten quickly punctured it by chewing rather than sucking. Then I learned that it was possible to squeeze the plastic bottle, thus forcibly ejecting the milk into the kitten's mouth, though this method did not make for an altogether relaxed mealtime. Fortunately the situation was resolved a few days later when I discovered in the dime store plastic doll bottles. On these the bobcats sucked as contentedly as any baby.

When they were three weeks old, we began to wean them to raw horse meat, a form of nourishment they much preferred to milk; but we could not tempt them with anything else, not even with such delicacies as kidney or liver. Later we learned, from someone experienced in the raising of wild animals, that bobcats will take to raw chicken provided it is presented to them when they are still very young. The proper diet of these animals is a problem, for when removed from their mother's milk they are particularly susceptible to rickets. One veterinarian told us of how the bones of one such young animal brought to him for treatment were so brittle that it could scarcely jump down from a chair without suffering a fracture.

Even after weaning, our bobcats never gave up their love of rubber nipples. In fact these became such an obsession that whenever they found one of our youngest's bottles, they would drag it off to some quiet place, such as the living-room couch, or better yet our bed, and chew on the nipple until it was demolished and they themselves were lying in a cold puddle of milk. If I discovered them so occupied and tried to remove the bottle, the cat would growl in what I judged to be a threatening manner. When I complained, my husband would comfort me by saying: "But dear, not everyone is so lucky as to have bobcats living with them."

At first the kittens lived in a box in our bathroom, but soon they were straying all over the house, and we were apt to come upon a lost ball of fluff squawking loudly for its brother almost anywhere. We called one Pluto after the King of Hades, which seemed to be a suitably sinister name for a bobcat, and to the other male we gave the kenning "Earchewer" in the Norse fashion, because he developed the habit of sucking on his brother's ear. The third we never named, referring to her simply as The Little Female. This was not due to any misogynous tendencies, but because she had few endearing features that would win her a place and name in our household. It was interesting to us how those three wild creatures evidenced so quickly three entirely different personalities. Earchewer preferred us to our dogs, Pluto preferred our dogs to us, and The Little Female would have nothing to do with any of us. Therefore she shortly went on exhibit at the Museum.

From left to right: The Little Female, Pluto, and Earchewer

Mornings for the bobkittens were often spent reducing our bedroom to shambles and afternoons in sleeping it off. A house arranged for small boys is probably fairly well arranged for bobcats, but a few modifications are needed. We have a large planter between the dining room and living room where hung our parrot cage. This was to give the bird the happy illusion that he was still in the jungle. However at times the illusion was too convincing, for the parrot would look down and see one or two tigerish creatures climbing up the rubber tree towards him. They also climbed up the moss-padded stakes that supported the philodendron. Whether this was in order to reach the parrot or because they wanted the exercise we were never able to determine precisely, but the threat, if one existed, was easily eliminated by tying segments or joints of cholla cactus onto all that was climbable. That kept the bobcats out of the branches, only they then decided that the planter itself was an admirable toilet. So we had to enclose the whole thing in chicken wire, and thus it remains.

Bobcats also climb Christmas trees. We had just finished decorating our first and had settled down to supper when from that direction came a horrendous crash. The bobcats, tantalized by the bright balls and lights, had been frolicking in the branches until they tipped the tree over. After repairing it we surrounded it with red paper which we covered with our trusty cholla cat-proofer, and far enough out so that the cats couldn't even reach a branch to bat at a ball, Scrooges that we were. This had the added advantage of also keeping crawling children and dogs at a distance. With such minor adjustments our house has survived both boys and other animals.

Pluto and our German shepherd

At this time we not only had two dogs, but a domestic cat as well, an ordinary black and white cat called Philip, a cat-cat, as we described him in the family idiom. He had mysteriously appeared out of the desert one morning in time for breakfast and stayed. Cats must have developed an effective underground, for several years later when Philip disappeared another black and white cat came to take his place. We called the newcomer Tobermory in memory of Saki's famous talking cat, and he is still with us.

Our bobcats took the ordinary household animals very much in their stride, though the first meetings were somewhat ticklish affairs. Let us say that Pluto is taking a morning stroll through the living room and suddenly comes upon a large black mountain lying in the middle of the rug. The mountain wags its tail and opens its mouth in a friendly smile. Pluto springs back in amazement, then stiff-legged, with his fur on end and his handsome Elizabethan ruff sticking out, he cautiously approaches until the dog and he are touching noses. During the cat's fearsome performance, the dog lies still with her head on the floor, her eyes rolling in apprehension, trying to look as ingratiating and harmless as possible. In reality, this is not any different from any get-acquainted ritual between a dog and a cat. But it is always surprising to see a wild animal demonstrate the familiar actions of a long domesticated one, though actually it is the reverse that should surprise one more, such as when a domestic cat paws at the floor in futile effort to cover the food left in the dish. The bobkittens even trained themselves to a cat box, so well, in fact, that when nature called and they were outside, they would rush in to use their box. We once had a bobcat that used the toilet, probably owing to the observed trait of bobcats defecating in water. And another one of ours particularly liked irrigated flowerbeds.

Our domestic cat, Philip, ignored his wild cousins, though occasionally he indulged in a brief romp with them, or allowed them to wash him, and Earchewer he permitted to suck the fur on

Pluto and Earchewer wrestling with our German shepherd

his stomach. A full-grown bobcat nursing a small *male* domestic cat was an absurd sight. Not having a thumb, the bobcat must have found Philip's fur a good substitute; and of course, as their mother, I felt guilty that Earchewer had not had enough sucking as a baby.

Our German shepherd and the bobcats became fast friends, enlivening our evenings with noisy boisterous games of chase, hide-and-seek, and wrestling. The dog would engulf a cat's head in her mouth, the cats would grab hold of the dog's legs, her ears, or her tail, and around and around they would go. All of our bobcats—and we have raised more than a half-dozen over the years—have taken not only to our domestic pets, but to our other wild ones as well. We have had them with ravens, a wolf, and a coyote. Mostly each goes his own way. Our oldest son Peter once had a small box turtle living with him which did lead a dubious life, as the bobcat liked to carry it around in his mouth. The turtle did not fancy this at all, becoming even more withdrawn than I think a turtle is supposed to be.

Before long Earchewer and Pluto were using the cat door and beginning to explore the outside. They never became very adept tree climbers, though sometimes they would venture up one after Philip or our boys. Their descent was more awkward than their ascent, scrabbling down with much noise and embarrassment. On the whole bobcats do not personify feline grace and their large-footed stance is often that of a gawky adolescent.

What our two bobcats did in the desert I do not know. I suppose they carried on the regular bobcat activities of hunting and sleeping. Sometimes I saw them sitting meditatively under a bush or caught glimpses of them walking along. Once I came upon Earchewer playing with a ground squirrel much as a cat plays with a mouse, tossing it up high into the air and then catching it. A bobcat's coloring is very protective and it is hard to distinguish

Earchewer yawning

him from his surroundings. A visiting University of California zoologist spent a morning stalking Earchewer in an effort to determine what possible purpose the conspicuous white marks on the backs of his ears might serve. Earchewer politely ignored him, continuing to walk about the desert in his usual lordly fashion. The only conclusion that the zoologist came to was that perhaps his ears were an example of disruptive coloration—a discontinuity of a pattern to better blend with the lights and shadows of the background.

Pluto and Earchewer lived with us for two and a half years, coming and going as they pleased. We kept a record of their activities and the odd thing was that they didn't always come and go together. As they grew older they spent longer stretches of time outside, sometimes almost a week. When they returned, usually in time for breakfast, they would retire to the living room for a long sleep. Earchewer liked the upholstered back of a chair on

Hugh and Penthesilea

which he sprawled with his legs dangling down on either side, and his brother would curl up in the seat below him.

Bobcats sleep in an abandoned and disorderly fashion compared to domestic cats. We had one who liked the crack between the two seat cushions of the sofa where he would lie on his back with his head hanging over the edge. Another preferred a particular planter in which he would sleep for hours, his chin propped on the rim and his legs spilling out. Our present bobcat sleeps mostly on her side with her paws bunched together in a tangle, or perhaps one long hind leg stretched out to serve as a chin rest. I have never seen a bobcat sleep with his front paws tucked neatly under him in that trancelike Buddha pose common to house cats.

Not the least of a bobcat's charms is his looks, graced as he is with an elegant ermine stomach and a tawny coat showing pale cinnamon when ruffled. A dinner guest, articulating ecstatically over their external appearances while lovingly stroking Earchewer, concluded her remarks with ". . . and what a beautiful rug your bobcats would make!" to which my husband answered sweetly, "Not more so than that pretty white dog of yours."

The bobcat's ears, as I have mentioned, are tipped with long black tufts and his face is tigerish with large round yellow eyes, owl eyes, whose pupils even when they contract show only a trace of the typical feline slit. His hind legs are noticeably longer than his front ones, which gives his back an upward slope ending in an impudent tail about five inches long, fuzzy and soft. This tail leads an independent life of its own, jerking and twitching constantly. Its tip is almost always slightly curled up, showing a touch of the white underside, unlike that of his larger cousin, the lynx, whose tail-tip is all black. Somehow, now that I am accustomed to bobcats, the ordinary cat's long tail seems very *déclassé*. I think the bobcats feel this way too, for they never fail to swipe at the domestic cat's tail should he carelessly leave it dangling over the edge of a chair.

Bobcats have a distinctive way of greeting each other. They

sing a quick, little chirping song and then turn and present to each other their tails held boldly upright. This is how they also sometimes greet a human being, and if one jumps in my lap while I am reading, he tickles my nose with his tail. What my response should be, other than to act as pleased as another bobcat, I have never been able to determine, but I try at least to make a similar noise, and though to my ears it sounds woefully inadequate, it seems to satisfy the cat.

Though we were delighted with these additions of ours, the same cannot be said of our respective in-laws, who watched the bobcats' growing size with alarm, wondering if we were not irresponsibly exposing our children to dreadful danger. A newspaper article describing in lurid detail how a little boy had had his toes eaten off by the pet ocelot almost caused hysteria in their ranks. The fact that the bobcats never made any overtly unfriendly gestures toward the boys comforted the relatives not in the least. "Someday," they would say, shaking their heads gloomily, "they will turn on you, or worse yet, on those poor defenseless little boys. What then?" And hardly a guest goes by who doesn't express the same sentiments by asking, "How long can you keep them? Aren't you afraid they will suddenly revert?"

This is an ancient prejudice held even by that wise old Greek Aeschylus:

> There was a shepherd who reared at home
> A lion's cub. It shared with sucking lambs
> Their milk—gentle, while bone and blood were young.
> The children loved it; the old watched and smiled.
> . . . But in time
> It showed the nature of its kind. Repaying
> Its debt for food and shelter, it prepared
> A feast unbidden. Soon the nauseous reek
> Of torn flesh filled the house. . . .
> The whelp once reared with lambs, now grown a beast,
> Fulfils his nature as Destruction's priest!

Bill has a theory about all of this. According to him a bobcat will not revert or return to a former state because he has never left that state. Though living in our house with us, a bobcat is still a wild animal; we do not "tame" him in the sense of trying to change his essential nature. All we can do is to wait and see if his nature is such that he can fit into our household without undue strain and we can live with him as he is. It becomes evident whether he will work out or not when he is hardly more than a kitten.

In the face of our experiences it would seem that V. H. Cahalane, a distinguished mammalogist, was unlucky when it came to raising bobcats, for he wrote in his book *Mammals of North America:*

Few . . . [bobcats] . . . ever become friendly or tolerant of their human captors. Even when captured as an impressionable and still-blind kitten, it is likely to be resentful and sullen. I have kept several bob-

cats and never found them friendly. Some were coldly aloof, some became contemptuously tolerant, while others remained openly resentful.

Earlier he describes a bobcat in the wild as seeming to be at first

. . . a timid animal that runs at the slightest provocation. When cornered or attacked by enemies, it becomes a different creature, a wild demon with unlimited courage. It screams, growls, spits, hisses, makes horrible faces, and tries to scratch out the eyes and every other part of the enemy's anatomy. . . . It is a wild and ferocious warrior.

I read this one evening and looked down with astonishment at the dozing Earchewer curled in my lap. Who would have believed all those things of that purring creature whose head was resting on my arm. Yet I knew that terror could transform him into a "wild demon," for this is logical and predictable behavior when an animal's security is threatened. However, it is highly unlikely that a bobcat will suddenly become mean or "turn" without cause.

Only once can I remember a bobcat becoming vicious—when Earchewer brought in a ground squirrel and proceeded to consume it on the dining-room table. Superficially this might seem to be an appropriate spot, but I thought that he should do his rodent-eating outside, attempting to persuade him of this with a gentle push of a broom. Earchewer growled ominously, his eyes narrowed, his ears flattened, and he swatted at the broom with such force that he knocked it out of my hand, at which point I quickly decided that he could eat his ground squirrel wherever he pleased. When I recounted this to my husband, he said, "You can't find fault with a bobcat defending his prey, though conceivably you might object if he were eating one of the boys."

As the years went by and the boys and the bobcats lived in happy association, our families' fears gradually faded. One particular afternoon our third son, who was still at the crawling stage, came clumping down the hall making a good deal of noise, as his legs were encased in heavy casts. A bobcat trailed him stealthily. Into the living room he crawled where my mother and a friend of hers were having tea. As he rounded the couch and made his way towards a large plateful of cookies, the bobcat sprang, landing on the child's back. This, being a routine procedure, did not in the least disturb Michael, who kept on without a pause, the bobcat clinging to him as to a rocking ship. But the guest, an elderly lady, almost fainted. Not so my mother, who went on pouring the tea as if nothing out of the ordinary had happened, which it hadn't. The guest was still shaking at her departure and tearfully muttered something about that poor child in those dreadful casts and then subjected to such cruel treatment by a ferocious wild animal. My mother unavailingly tried to reassure her that quite to the contrary, Michael and the cat loved each other and the pouncing game was their favorite.

A similar episode took place one evening when we had a distinguished zoologist from the East as a dinner guest. He watched the performance with fascination, smacked his lips and said, "This is indeed a most interesting experiment that you are conducting!"

A bobcat is as playful as any cat, but just because he is larger and more rugged than a domestic one does not mean that he can be played with more roughly. Actually the reverse is true. My husband disapproves of rough-housing with wild animals, or even of actively encouraging them to play, for as with young children, games that are too exuberant can quickly become out of hand, and what starts out as fun may trigger reactions other than play. Also, as he grows stronger, a bobcat can use his teeth and claws in a way that only he considers to be playful!

A friend of ours once said that you don't have to have wit to live in this country, circumstances provide whatever entertainment you might need. Certainly our bobcats have provided an enormous amount of circumstantial material to amuse us. For example there was the morning that Bill went off to work as usual, reappearing shortly with a bobcat in the back of his car. He dashed into the house with a struggling Earchewer under his arm, deposited him in the study, all the while spinning a complicated tale about how he was driving down the road when he noticed a bobcat sitting on top of a telephone pole. Not knowing whether this was one of ours or a wild one, he slammed on his brakes, jumped out, and called, "Here pussy, here pussy." The creature on top of the pole made no response, but Earchewer appeared from under a mesquite. So Bill concluded that the poled bobcat was Pluto.

Next he called the telephone company. "Hello, this is William Woodin on Cloud Road and my cat is stuck up on the top of one of your poles . . . yes . . . yes . . . That would be fine. Thank you and please tell him I'll be waiting for him by the pole." With that he grabbed a pan of horsemeat and rushed out of the house to the garage from which he reappeared with a long stick at one end of which he had fastened a noose. All this equipment he put into the car and drove off.

I piled the boys into my car and followed. We arrived just before the telephone truck. A neat young man climbed out of it and came over to where I was standing. We watched Bill brandishing the dish of horsemeat over his head and calling, "Here pussy!" This had no effect on Pluto, so Bill rattled the pan on a nearby stone, which was how he summoned them in for their breakfast if they were outside. Pluto continued to sit soundlessly and unmoving, glumly staring down at us. The telephone man turned to me and muttered uncertainly in a low voice, "Say, is that an ordinary cat? Looks kinda funny to me."

"No," I replied, "that is one of our bobcats."

The neat little man looked more uncertain than ever. "Never saw one of those before. I'm from Ohio. Is he tame?"

"Oh, yes, very tame," said I reassuringly.

At this point Bill was getting the stick out of the car. Then he joined us and asked the man, "Do you have a ladder in your truck?"

"Yes," answered the man, "and you're most welcome to use it.

I'm not very good with cats. They don't like me." He got out the ladder, set it up, and retreated. I held the bottom of the ladder while Bill climbed to where he could reach Pluto with the stick. Pluto was now snarling and spitting. The telephone man climbed into his truck and closed the door. Bill dropped the noose over Pluto's head and swung him to the ground. Then he himself scrambled down and pushed the struggling and furious cat into the car. After the door was safely shut, the telephone man ventured out of his truck to retrieve his ladder and drove off shaking his head. Perhaps "back home" looked better to him now than it had yesterday.

Another time, when our cats had been gone for several weeks, I glimpsed a bobcat crossing the road and called the radio-telephone operator who served the Museum, which was without regular service, asking her to relay what I had seen to my husband. An hour later the operator called back with his answer. "He says for you to go to where you saw the bobcat and to call 'Pussy, pussy, pussy'—at least that is what I think he said, but that sure doesn't sound right!" We never saw our cats again.

Our next bobcat also came to us as a tiny kitten. It was extremely shy and stayed, during its brief sojourn at our house, under our bed. It came out only long enough to eat and to give us all ringworm. This inglorious disease is not only a nuisance but is astoundingly tenacious. After having fruitlessly made the rounds of the dermatologists, in despair I went to our veterinarian. Not until my name was called out by the receptionist and I marched into the inner sanctum with three small boys, did I notice the bewildered expressions of the rest of the clientele who were waiting with their dogs and cats. They must have been wondering if they should tell me I was in the wrong office.

Then came Diana. She arrived already named and half-grown. Immediately we found having only one cat made a great difference, for it would turn to us for companionship instead of to its brothers or sisters. Diana adored the boys, following them around like a dog. She particularly loved to take baths with them, which was our first experience with a bobcat's fascination with water. She would sit on the edge of the tub and bat the water or their moving toes. She also liked to lick their wet hair. This same cat often paddled in the stream with the boys as they built dams or sailed their boats. Diana insisted on sleeping with the baby, and sometimes when I went in to cover him she would be occupying the major part of the bed, having pushed the baby way over to one side.

The time came when we thought Diana ought to be spayed, on the theory that this would help to ensure her good nature and keep her from wandering. During the discussion of this matter, the boys naturally asked for an explanation. Peter, then six, listened carefully to the why's and wherefore's of the operation and then made a pronouncement. "Well, I think we should have mother spayed also."

Like our previous bobcats, Diana was allowed to come and go as she wished. Infallibly she accompanied us on our walks and

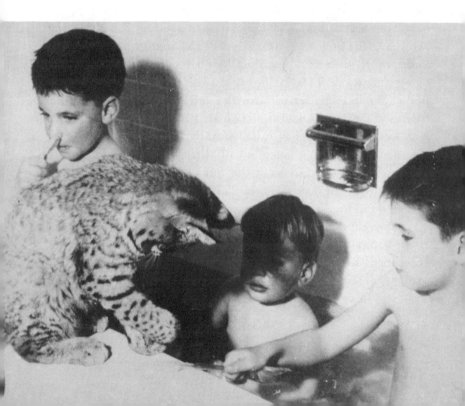

picnics, and insisted on being included in all of our activities, whether we were raking leaves or gardening or painting or climbing trees or making mud pies. Nothing was too menial or trivial for her not to wish to be part of, and the enthusiasm with which she joined group activities would have made any kindergarten teacher beam with pleasure, a subject upon which I will later enlarge.

During her first summer, when she was a little over a year old, the boys and I went to visit my mother, leaving the house empty during the day. Diana missed the boys, and being used to lots of company and activity, she took to the desert in hopes of finding some there. One day she did not come home for her supper and we never saw her again. I do not like to think about what might have happened to her. Now we keep our bobcats inside.

On Diana's heels, one after another, came Tamberlane, Martin, and Penthesilea. We inclined towards naming our bobcats after fierce and famous warriors such as they themselves were supposed to be. Tammy disappeared into the desert as had his predecessors, Martin died of an incurable disease, and Penny developed what we thought then was a strange habit of expressing her affection by wetting all over the furniture. A member of the Museum staff who adored bobcats and was an almost furnitureless bachelor, offered her a home. We have since learned that such behavior is not uncommon in bobcats.

Now we have Tiger Balm whom we call Tiggy. She is more nervous of the children than our others, as she does not like their noise or sudden movements, and she is also timid with strangers. Our others, if they liked people, liked all people, but Tiggy discriminates, which I find flattering. During the day when the boys are in school and in the evening when they have gone to bed, she runs madly all over the house, teasing our domestic cat, teasing the snakes in their cages, playing with her rubber squeaky mouse and stuffed animals, fishing in the aquarium if I have forgotten to cover it. She will jump onto the table where I am working, chew my pencil, pounce on my papers, knock my eraser onto the floor, and then finally she sits plunk in the middle of where I am trying to write and stares at me with those large unblinking yellow eyes. In those eyes I see my face reflected and I wonder if she sees herself in mine and if this is what gives us our sense of affinity, so that for a suspended second I am not sure where the cat leaves off and I begin.

If she is dozing and I walk by, she will wake up, rush off in front of me, and then sprawl on the floor, rolling over so that I can rub her stomach. Or she will wind herself in and out of my legs, begging to be noticed. Bobcats are far more affectionate than domestic cats, liking and wanting attention whenever you're around and not just at mealtimes. When she wants company and knows we are behind the closed door, she will make a harsh Siamese-like meow which, outside of the greeting chirp, a purr, and a growl, is the only other sound we hear her make. I am sure though, that among themselves in the wild their language is much more varied. After all, here no one can teach Tiggy her proper language.

In the evening when I read she jumps on my lap and nestles down for a nap with her head resting on my knee. Or she may walk along the upholstered back of my chair and, after a nibble or two, settle behind my neck, until she spies Toby, our domestic cat. Then she is off to entice him to play, with a tentative pat of her paw. Toby is never enthusiastic over such an invitation; he would much rather sleep, and should he continue to ignore her, Tiggy will either present him with her rubber mouse as added inducement or will simply pounce on him. Occasionally Tiggy will be content to lie beside him, and after washing his face and ears for him, will also nap a while.

First thing in the morning, when my husband opens our bedroom door, Tiggy will rush in to play. She jumps on our toes, our stomachs, our heads, and chews whatever moves. Sometimes she brings her rubber mouse with her in hopes that we will play with it too. Her games soon exhaust us but never her.

I have grown tired of a cat box in the bathroom, so the other day I knocked a hole through the wall under my dressing table and outside we built a large pen. Tiggy was delighted with this new arrangement. She not only uses it for its intended purpose, but she will sit out there in the early morning to watch the birds, and at night she listens.

Last week a new man from the termite control company came to inspect. He suddenly appeared from our bedroom looking popeyed and shaken. "I was on my hands and knees looking under the desk," he explained, "when I heard a funny noise and there, staring down at me, was this huge animal with big yellow eyes."

"Oh, that's just our bobcat," I reassured him. "She won't hurt you."

As I have mentioned, bobcats are exuberant participants in almost any activity you might care to name. Not even a toddler can make his presence more forcibly known than can a congenial bobcat, whether it is in a flowerbed you are attempting to weed or in a picnic basket. I suspect that a number of Tucson parents will long remember a certain Easter egg hunt down by our stream that was also attended by Diana. Full of high spirits, Diana pursued the children who were pursuing the eggs, pursued the children who were paddling in the shallow water, investigated lunch baskets, paper sacks, and the rubbish pile, and finally she was discovered by an apprehensive mother just as she was cuddling down for a nap by the side of her young son tucked away in a bassinet.

Over the years I have learned that certain things cannot be accomplished in the presence of a bobcat. One cannot make a bed, and as for changing a bed, well, it's a disaster. One cannot go to sleep, for the incessant purr next to one's ear is like a loud motor. One cannot sew on a sewing machine, or set the table, or arrange flowers in a vase. In fact it is unlikely that one can even have a vase of flowers around. Diana favored daffodils, to chew that is, though as yet Tiggy has shown no such preferences. She likes to nibble on them all, pull them out of their container, and then dabble in the water. Bobcats are even more dedicated water-dabblers than are small boys.

Therefore one cannot wash dishes, and when it comes to a bath-tub full of water, why the mere sight of it sends Tiggy into paroxysms of joy. In two seconds she has fished out the rubber tub-mat as well as the washcloth, and after knocking the soap into the water, she spends many jolly minutes chasing it around and around. What a bobcat leaping in and out of a large amount of water will do to a bathroom is all too easily imagined. One of my favorite personal indulgences is a languid bath in which I can stretch out, soak, and day-dream, but a barely submerged body is a challenge to Tiggy. She will sit on the edge of the tub and pat at a knee or foot, shaking each huge paw in my face as it gets wet. Then she will try and walk along a leg as one might an underwater log, until she reaches higher ground, say my chest, and there she will sit staring down at me with a smile that would put to shame both the Sphinx and the Mona Lisa.

The other day she discovered Toby's cat door and went boldly out it. On noticing her absence a short time later, we searched the desert around the house without being able to find her. We were afraid that, being unfamiliar with the desert, she might not be able to find her way home should she wander too far. The next morning, just before dawn, I heard a loud purr beside my ear. "Tiggy's back!" I muttered sleepily to my husband, who leaped out of bed to nail up the cat door.

To fill his insatiable need for company man has spent centuries meddling with cats and dogs. Without a doubt he has produced a reliable and serviceable creature, but one far less interesting now than was his ancient ancestor. This, of course, is a prejudice of ours, but I am willing to bet that anyone who has had a wild animal living with him will agree. Sometimes I am asked what this is like, to live with a wild animal, and then I think of those black tufted ears and the large golden eyes that turn to look at me, and I think it is keeping lordly company. I think of those peculiar pulsating moments when we confront each other, eye to eye, and I feel in her tensed muscles and twitching tail a flow of life quite independent of my own and yet akin to it. With a wild animal there is no question of ownership, nor is the relationship one of master to servant, of superior to inferior; it is an equal affair, equally given. A mutual curiosity always lurks, and perhaps a slight wariness, as neither of us is absolutely sure what the other's reaction will be; and on my side comes an insatiable desire to hear the voices that speak to her secretly and by which she lives. To watch a bobcat and a small boy climbing around in a tree together, to sit by the edge of a stream and share a sandwich with a raven, to shiver beside a coyote because the night is wet and cold, is to be reminded that we are all entangled in the long dark sigh of life, which is at once a wonder and a comfort.

John with his kingsnake in a mesquite tree

5

Snakes
(and other misunderstood friends)

SNAKES link happy and eager hands with both small boys and the desert (if I can sneak an unscientific description past my husband). Either boys or the desert will produce snakes, and a combination of the two will produce three times as many. There is never a time but that at least one son has one snake in his room. And somewhere in the house at least one lizard lives a jaunty life of catching flies on a window sill.

That the desert comes equipped with snakes is no surprise. They take their necessary place in the scheme of things by serving as food for certain birds, large mammals, and other snakes, and in turn by eating different birds, smaller mammals, lizards, and other snakes. That small boys come equipped with snakes is less easy either to accept or to explain. Nothing in my own childhood has been of any help in my understanding their preoccupation with this form of life. I cannot remember being particularly revolted nor particularly fascinated by snakes. They just lived in the woods and fields along with the birds, bugs, and other things and were consequently part of the background I used in my games and imaginings.

As a twentieth century, Geselled mother of sons, I vaguely realized that one of the real pleasures of boyhood is to shock.

Boys quickly learn that the risk of later painful unpleasantness is lessened if they shock with something they have rather than by something they do, and instinctively they know that although shrunken heads or rotting bones do produce satisfactory results, animate objects work better than inanimate ones. A brief review of the animals they might conceivably be able to possess for their Machiavellian purposes eliminates such items as hyenas and vampire bats, and they decide on either mice, rats, spiders, or snakes, any of which is sure to rouse a cry of horror from some female whatever her size or age. Of these varmints the snake is the most easily kept and produces the most reliable results.

Another possibility, of course, is that boys simply like to have pets, and snakes make good pets. They are clean, neat, quiet, and odorless, and best of all, they need to be fed only every two weeks in the summer and not at all during the winter months, providing they are kept reasonably cool so that their metabolism slows down. They do not run about scratching at doors or barking to be let in or out, they do not urinate on rugs, they do not chew things to pieces, they do not scratch their claws on the furniture, and they can be carried around easily in hand or pocket. They are even pettable, though they cannot be considered even by Old Mother West Wind to be affectionate. But what they lack in warmth they make up in convenience, and for a boy who has to care for his pet himself, this is a proper consideration. I have made only three rules governing the keeping of snakes. The boys may not keep, nor even catch, poisonous ones; all snake cages must be kept in their own rooms; and snakes cannot be brought to the dining-room table. This last rule I added after seeing, one mealtime, a long black head poking out of Peter's shirt pocket and two beady eyes staring at me from across the table. Admittedly rule number three may be unreasonable, but mothers have their little idiosyncrasies that need to be humored.

I was about to spend some time speculating as to why little girls do not also keep snakes for pets but then I remembered being told that little girls keep pets primarily for the purpose of dressing them up in doll clothes and taking them for walks in tiny perambulators. In spite of its many virtues, the snake's one failing is that it will not look cute in a doll bonnet and dress. Besides I have heard that little girls are afraid of snakes.

The fear of snakes does make for interesting speculation. Why is it that a snake is so repugnant to so many people? He is not ugly like a bat nor is he slimy like an eel; he doesn't smell like a skunk nor is he noisy like a parrot. In fact his firm round body is satisfying to hold and his cool dry smooth skin is pleasantly touchable. And he is beautiful to watch as he slides sinuously over the ground, a long distillation of grace. Anyone who saw *The Living Desert* will remember the brilliant red-white-and-black banded shovel-nosed snake that flowed in and out of the sand in such lovely liquid curves. That particular snake happened to belong to my husband. It was not dancing ecstatically as one might have supposed; instead it was desperately trying to get away from the too-hot lamps and died shortly afterwards.

The fear of snakes, my husband explains, is completely learned. It is handed down from generation to generation as are secret recipes and family heirlooms. A properly brought up child will have a good healthy attitude towards snakes, meaning that he will like them. Certainly our four boys have no such fear and I remember vividly the time Bill needed someone to hold his mountain kingsnake while he photographed it. At that moment no one was about but one-year-old Peter, so he thrust the snake into his son's hands. Though it was the first snake that Peter had ever held or even seen, he showed not a tinge of repugnance or fright. He crowed with delight as it squirmed in his fingers, and with his free hand tried to touch the darting tongue. But I bet at least one reader is shuddering by now if he is not actively sick to his stomach.

How illogical are such fears was well illustrated the evening that my husband found himself sitting at a dinner table between two women one of whom hated spiders but did not mind mice and the other of whom hated mice but did not mind spiders. And neither of them was afraid of snakes, or so they said!

In all honesty it is only fair to point out that one problem does exist to the keeping of snakes. These creatures have an outstanding characteristic common to them all: no matter how well confined they inevitably escape. During the years of my husband's growing up his snakes escaped in cars, trains, closets of relatives, and in foreign cities. To allow a son to "fool around" with snakes takes stamina; to support his interest, as did his mother, takes wisdom. Whenever Bill's family gather together, a tale involving one or another of his Houdini-like snakes is sure to be brought out of the storeroom of family memories. These have come to assume the position of the familiar and beloved bedtime story and the boys often will ask: "Do tell us about the time Daddy's python escaped in India," or "I want to hear about the mother garter snake who had fifty-two babies behind the books in the library," or "What did Gramma say when the snake crawled into the beautiful antique sofa?" or "What happened when Grandad lassoed the alligator in the neighbor's swimming pool?"

And so we all crowd together on the couch and I begin: "Once upon a time when your father was a boy, a bit bigger than Michael and a bit smaller than John, he had a large and lovely snake. A gopher snake it was, and its name was Charley. It was three feet long and lived in a cage in the playroom, but from there it was apt to wander . . ." And when I have finished and the boys are thinking dreamily about when their father was no bigger than they, sometimes they will ask me, "And you, Mother, didn't you have any snakes to keep you company when you were young?"

It is not strange that snakes should figure in children's bedtime stories, for through the centuries they have starred in legends, literature, religions, and plain tall tales. Ever since Eve snakes have been showered with attention, most of it detrimental to their health and happiness. A refreshingly different attitude from our

John and two kingsnakes

own towards these maligned animals has been displayed for centuries by the Hopi Indians who live in the desert of northeastern Arizona. They believe that the snake acts as a vital messenger between their priests and the all-important rain gods by carrying their prayers for rain down to them in the underworld. It is curious to note that Hermes, Zeus's sportive messenger who was charged with leading the souls of the dead to Hades, carried in his hand the caduceus, a winged stick entwined by serpents.

The Hopi Snake Dance has become a popular summer attraction for tourists as well as for herpetologists. The tourists, willing to believe in magic and mystery, speculate as to whether the rattlers that the priests carry between their teeth are in their natural state or have been defanged or milked of their venom, while the herpetologists speculate only as to which method has been used to render them harmless. At the conclusion of the ceremony the snakes, sometimes numbering over a hundred and including several species, are turned loose and presumably hurry off to deliver the rain petitions.

The incredible feats that our own culture attributes to snakes seem hardly less remarkable and a good deal less serviceable. Milk snakes are believed to milk cows, stealing as much as a quart at a sitting, hoop snakes to grab their own tails in their mouths and go rolling down hillsides, and mother snakes to swallow their young in the face of danger, disgorging them when all is once again safe. I have some sympathy for the tellers of such tales, for I can remember peering out of a window to where my husband's two pythons were undulating in his family's pool, heads raised to enjoy the view. To me, safely inside, they looked as if they were breathing fire and were at least as long as the Mississippi.

Though people think they hate snakes, and whenever they see one, harmless or poisonous, they will kill it, they love to hear about them. At a snake lecture the degree of audience enjoyment can be measured by the number of slightly heaving, knotted sacks spread out before the lecturer. Of this fact Bill, who began to lecture at twelve, soon became aware and he never disappoints his listeners. He is a master of suspense. "Arizona is particularly fortunate in having more different kinds of snakes than almost any other state in the union," he will say, casually indicating the wriggling sacks beside him. A few minutes later, he picks up the first sack, and absentmindedly strokes it. "A snake's strongest sense is the sense of smell." He puts the first sack down, picks up another and begins to untie the knot. "Since the tongue itself cannot smell, it brings particles from the air into the mouth where a special smelling organ is located. . . . Snakes have backward curving teeth, as I will show you shortly, which help them to keep hold of their prey while they eat it." With the sack at last untied he reaches down into it and feels around. The sack dances and shakes. "Snakes do not chew their food, preferring to swallow their victims whole, which sometimes is an arduous and time-consuming task. Because of the special construction of the jaw a snake can open his mouth wide enough to accommodate a meal surprisingly bigger in circumference than he is himself." And while the audience is digesting this fact he suddenly holds up the lecture's first specimen, a six-foot gopher snake.

But in order to show or keep snakes, they first have to be caught. Snake collecting is a relatively unknown art with techniques and idioms that set it apart from ordinary human activities and clothe it with a certain mystery. I am reminded of a family anecdote involving my husband's grandmother, who once watched the herpetologist from the American Museum of Natural History catch a snake in her garden and exclaimed, "So that's how it's done. You just grab them behind the ears," a remark that elicited from my husband, then seven, a lengthy lecture on how snakes do not have external ears. That story has always stuck in my mind and I am rather inclined to think that, in spite of the physiological inaccuracies, Bill's grandmother very well described the catching of snakes. I hasten to add, of harmless snakes.

Poisonous snakes necessitate a different approach. When he

has one available, my husband uses a snake stick. This is a four-foot-long handle with a T-shaped bar fastened to one end. With this the snake's head is held down so that it can be picked up "behind the ears," or more accurately, on the head itself so that the snake cannot twist around and bite you. Snakes are sneaky and it is well to remember this. If, as well as a snake stick, you have a snake box (a stout box with a hinged lid and a large lock) or some other suitable container, you can simply lift the snake with the crook of the stick, where he will balance himself, and then drop him into the box.

If you do not have a bona fide snake stick at hand, you can use the branch of a tree or whatever will serve to pin down the animal's head securely to the ground. Don't use a forked stick. This imaginative detail that so often appears in fiction must have resulted in a number of snake-catching readers being bitten, for unless the fork fits tightly on the snake's head, it is obviously a precarious maneuver.

Snakes, whether in the wild or in one's house, have a way of threatening the smoothness and concord of life. They have an uncanny knack of providing excitement and, depending on the point of view, entertainment. It was not long after my marriage that I began to experience both.

During the two years that Bill was completing his undergraduate work at the University of Arizona in Tucson, we lived in a small adobe brick cottage with a red tiled roof. In the first weeks of playing house, snakes had been dismissed, even forgotten, by me. For one thing, our landlord, having heard of Bill's propensities, had his lawyer insert a small statement in the lease to the effect that no live reptiles could be housed on the premises. This, in my mind, was specific language, and I basked in the belief that at least while Bill was busy with textbooks I would be spared any further intimacy with snakes alive.

I couldn't have been more mistaken. One cool October morning such as the desert, after its blistering summer, assumes to revive its inhabitants, I extravagantly began one of Fanny Farmer's more puzzling experiments. I was still in the preliminary stages of trying to blanch nuts and extract the juice from two onions, when the doorbell rang. On our threshold was an agitated man holding gingerly at arm's length an embroidered pillow slip from whose innards came a gentle buzzing.

"Is Mr. Woodin in?"

"No, but can I help you?" (Polite words I have since learned to modify.)

"Well, I found this rattler in the chicken coop and I hear tell he collects the varmints, God help him! So here it is, Ma'am." With that he handed me the pillow slip and departed. I dropped it behind the door and waited in another room for my husband's return a few hours later. After my explanations of what had happened and why it was I wouldn't come out of the bedroom, Bill went to remove the problem pillow slip and its contents to the car. A moment of silence ensued and then he reappeared with the pillow slip turned inside out. "Nothing here now," he said. "Are you sure there was a rattler in it?" The mixing together of

From left to right: Peter and gopher snake; Michael; John and kingsnake; and Hugh

one new bride and one loose rattlesnake in a small house is a recipe almost guaranteed not to produce connubial bliss.

Next I discovered that word of the landlord's ban had not been circulated throughout the reptile kingdom, and while cleaning one day I found an uninvited caller under the couch. I carefully scrutinized the eleven inches of snake from across the room and decided that he was a gopher snake . . . harmless, of kindly disposition, and of service to the farmer by consuming numerous mice, rats, and other destructive rodents. Or so said the book. Now, thought I, I shall distinguish myself forever by catching this noble specimen. It took a half hour of trepidatory jockeying with a fly swatter and a coat hanger before I managed to deposit my prey into a wastebasket. This I later presented to my husband much as a vassal might present his liege with a basilisk.

"And he hissed and wiggled and struck four times at the fly swatter!" said I, shivering at the memory. "Of kindly disposition, my eye!"

"Fly swatter!" said Bill as he peered into the wastebasket. "What on earth were you doing with a fly swatter? Didn't you just pick him up? He'll make an excellent meal for my kingsnake. Thanks, hon."

What a disappointment. Somehow I thought that my first specimen should have a more distinguished end than that of filling another snake's stomach.

These early dramas were by no means confined to our house and me. The snake business wears a mantle of strange adventure, and the meek and mild should pursue other pathways. One day the Museum received a telephone call from Mexico, the fabulous land of the snake-god Quetzalcoatl. A woman, in halting English, offered the Museum important specimens. They being reptilian, the job of driving down to the Mexican border town of Nogales, sixty-five miles south of Tucson, to collect them, fell to my husband.

He arrived at the designated hour at the designated hotel and, brushing past the swarms of boys and flies clustered at the entrance, he presented himself to a mustachioed swell who sat with his feet on the desk picking his teeth.

"I have an appointment to see Miss M.," said my husband briskly. The shiny-shoed Lothario surveyed him silently for a minute, without removing the toothpick from his teeth or his feet from the desk, and jerked his head towards the stairs, muttering a barely distinguishable "34."

Bill, who felt that it was unseemly to appear at a strange woman's bedroom door, even at eleven in the morning, knocked timidly. The door opened and a large woman stood before him whom he has since been able to describe only as well-stacked. She was wearing a violent cerise kimono and her long black hair strayed over much of its surface in curling tentacles. To Bill's announcement of his name and business, she said "Come in," or something approximating this, in a heavy accent, smiling and waving him past her through the fumes of gardenia scent.

As the door closed behind him, the snake charmer launched into an unbroken broken-English monologue describing the sinuous experiences of her trade. She revealed that she not only wished to give her beloved specimens to the Museum but herself as well, for she thought her act would prove irresistible on the Museum steps!

"Ah," she sighed. "You should have seen me in Paris." and from the way she . . . ah . . . rolled her eyes, she must have been a regular Nouvelle Eve. "I danced like thees and zee snake, he goes like thees, and then . . . pouf . . . he bite me! Vould you like to see zee scars?"

In August of that same year Bill's rarest rattler produced twelve young. A week later I managed to produce only one. Mine could not strike, slither away, or in any way defend itself except with loud screams. Such are the ways of the hapless human. When Bill gleefully pointed out the discrepancies between the mother rattler's young and mine, and how much more able and interesting one was than the other, I answered, "Yes, rattlesnakes are certainly very clever. How wonderful it would be if I too could produce twelve babies at one time. What a start towards a family that would be!"

My husband's attitude towards children is misleading if one judges it only by what he says. The first time the subject chanced to appear in our conversation was early in our marriage as he was eating his breakfast eggs. He quickly closed the subject by saying vaguely, "Well, I suppose one has them, like one has eggs for breakfast."

When he says, "I'll leave them alone if they'll leave me alone," he means that children should be children in their own world, he preferring to remain an adult in his (I think). And when a cocker puppy appeared in the wake of our first-born, he said, "You can have either trained dogs and untrained children, or trained children and untrained dogs, but we haven't the time for both." Fortunately I chose the second. His Al Cappian point of view, implemented by fairness and clearly understood discipline, has had excellent results, and thanks to him we have what I am told are four presentable sons.

After our more or less snakeless sojourn in Berkeley, we moved back to Tucson and into our own house. Snakes once again resumed their primary position in our lives. Well, almost. Now my husband had other diversions—livelier, fuzzier, warmer ones, such as bobcats, coyotes, ravens, and oh, yes, boys. The number of snake collectors duly increased to five, and each and every one of them, sons as well as father, seem to draw snakes out of the desert like a magnet. Several times I have come upon a small boy or two, usually barefoot, poised in fascination over what turns out to be a baby rattlesnake. One morning I almost put my hand on a rattlesnake that had chosen the second shelf in the carport storage cabinet as his winter resting place. And once I found a perfectly strange snake curled up asleep on the coffee table. He had simply come in from the outside and made himself at home, which leads me to surmise that, among their other gifts, snakes also have the ability to discover congenial surroundings. Perhaps, like hobos, they make a special mark on the doorstep as a sign to others passing by.

Once caught, snakes are no more apt now to stay put in their new home than they were in the days of my husband's childhood. Not long ago a brood of young kingsnakes escaped in the study and somehow got themselves into the ventilating system from which they reappeared at unlikely moments in unlikely places. It is in the boys' rooms, though, where most of the escapes occur. I'm still unable to decide whether I prefer to know of the disappearance and to be in a perpetual state of anxiety, or whether I prefer a state of ignorance and to run the risk of total surprise should I suddenly come upon the culprit in a bureau drawer.

We have caught some dozen or more rattlesnakes in the immediate environs of the house, a number of these in what I persist in thinking is a snakeproof play-yard. I am at my uneasiest about rattlesnakes in the spring and fall when they come out of or are hunting shelter, for it is then that we find most of them. If my husband overhears me warning the boys to be careful of rattlesnakes in what he deems to be an overly enthusiastic manner, he interrupts by saying that they must be taught respect, not fear, any more than one teaches them to be afraid of matches. "Well, then," I say, full of righteous indignation, "what would happen if one of the boys were bitten?"

"It depends on many factors," he answers, "—on how much venom was injected, the size and species of rattlesnake because some have a more potent venom than others, the location of the bite, the size, health, and sensitivity of the child—so I can't say. Besides, many more children are killed by being struck by cars than by rattlers. And if the boys are sensible and watch where they walk, they're not likely to be bitten."

No more specific is a discussion on how to treat the victim of snake bite. One school of thought advocates the classic "cut

John out hunting lizards to feed his snakes

and suck" technique, another the newer so-called "cryotherapy," or prolonged application of cold, and some think anti-venin indispensable, while others claim it often does more harm than good. Because of the possibility that long exposure to cold will damage tissue and yet because of its probable efficacy in retarding the absorption of the venom, my husband recommends a moderate combination of the two methods along with the judicious use of anti-venin.

Try and get a clear definite answer out of a scientist some day! Perhaps their problem is one of lost innocence so that they no longer can reflect the ambiguities simply, as can a child. Michael's recent Science report begins: "I think Science has something to do with life. Like how frogs live and where do they come from and what do they eat," and ends: "Caterpallars make a cocoon. When Spring comes they break the cocoon. Some of them are moths and others are butterflys. But they get no bigger than they are." A perfectly true and irreproachable concluding statement that should be the envy of anyone, zoologist or poet.

I still worry about rattlesnakes. To tell the truth, I hate them. I feel about them much the way the early settlers felt about the Indians—the only good one is a dead one.

I remember a field trip when Bill caught two large diamondback rattlers. The only available sack for the second was the sack in which the first was already imprisoned. I was to hold that sack open while Bill dropped the second snake into it. "No!" said I when I was informed of my role. "I won't!"

My husband looked at me in disbelief. "You mean you won't hold open the sack for me as any other herpetologist's wife would be glad to do for her husband?"

"No, I won't!"

"In heaven's name, why not? It's so simple! Any child could do it. I'll even unknot the sack for you and all you have to do is to stand there and hold it so that the other rattler doesn't come out while I drop this one in."

"I won't!" I repeated monotonously, retreating behind a saguaro. Bill glowered at me silently and silently stalked over to the car, opened the luggage compartment, and dropped the rattlesnake inside. And in silence we drove home, I with my feet well tucked up under me. The surprising thing is that I rode in the car at all. But then the alternative was not any more attractive, the nearest phone being a good ten miles away; and whom would I call, and what would I say?

Last fall Peter, who was out hunting lizards to feed his kingsnake, came running over the desert shouting excitedly. He appeared at the door holding up a snake bag which bulged ominously. "Look what I caught!" and with a flourish he laid the sack down on the grass, picked up its corners, and dumped out two large headless rattlesnakes.

"Look what I caught!" That triumphant male phrase rings down through the centuries, heralding victory. Sometimes he arrives dragging a dragon by the tail, or a saber-toothed tiger, or his mortal enemy the neighboring king. And the waiting female stands ready to exclaim over him, over his prize, whether it be the phoenix bird or two rattlesnakes with their heads shot off.

I remember the evening I was reading to the two older boys, who were each holding their respective snakes, a kingsnake and a gopher snake. The boys became so absorbed in the story that they forgot about their pets. I happened to glance down and there in my lap was the kingsnake in the process of swallowing the gopher snake.

At my screams and the boys' shouts of "Your snake is eating my snake!" "Do something!" "Oh, my poor snake. *You* do something!" Bill rushed in, grabbed the snakes and dropped them onto the floor. The kingsnake burped up the gopher snake, and the latter, none the worse for his brief immersion, crawled dazedly away. Peter picked up his snake and went off to his room scolding it, John picked up his snake and went off to his room comforting it, and I simply went off.

I remember a hot summer evening when we were sitting on the hill behind our house watching the lightning stab the mountains and I announced that the only way to be cool in this impossible climate was to sit forever in a cold bath, and that was just what I was going to do. "Excellent idea!" said my husband, and I remember noticing, in the dusk, a certain smile that had come to tell me, an interested wife, as much as did a certain flick of a bobcat's tail. Still, I was not prepared, and when I entered the bathroom I found the tub already occupied by three gopher snakes, two racers, and one large desert boa. Soaking snakes in water is one of the treatments for mites.

I remember the day a woman came to inspect us in answer to an ad for a housekeeper, announcing as she entered that not only did she hate snakes, but she couldn't even stand to see one. I assured her in my most confident manner that the few snakes we had around were kept locked in the study, in cages, and that no one went in there except my husband. That day Bill was slumped glumly in a chair, his right arm swollen and his right hand, even more hideously swollen, immersed in a pan of ice cubes. In the course of our discussion of country life, the desert, our habits, our kitchen and the duties attached to it, the boys, and the due date of our third child visibly bulging under my jacket, our prospective housekeeper whispered,

"What is the matter with Mr. Woodin?"

"Well," I said, and coughed, "he was cleaning the cage of one of his specimens and he thought it was asleep. Then it bit him and he's had a—a—slight reaction."

"What kind of a specimen was it?"

"Oh, a very small rattlesnake," I answered offhandedly. "A rare and interesting type that occurs only in the mountains at an altitude of over five thousand feet. Have you ever been up in our Arizona mountains in the fall when the aspen have turned?" But what I hoped would be a diverting question was lost as Bill, who had been gazing out the window, leaped out of his chair and dashed outside. Reaching into a small bush, which fortunately was hidden from our visitor's view, he extracted a garter snake and stuffed it into his pocket.

Our visitor maintained a bewildered silence, and when Bill reappeared I said brightly, "He must have suddenly remembered where he left his pocket knife," adding as he sauntered by, "Did you find your knife, dear?"

"Yes," he answered, "would you like to see it?" grinning wickedly.

The end of this story is a happy one. For ten years Mrs. Howay kept the keys, undaunted by the turbulence that our household could so readily, almost eagerly, produce. She firmly, though not always silently, stood her ground in the face of what is so glibly called "the unexpected": the large glassy eyes of a frozen owl in the deep freeze, lizards in the refrigerator waiting to be fed to snakes, the tarantula that popped out of my husband's lunch pail, scorpions in her bathtub, floods in the kitchen from a misdirected cloudburst, the raven that pulled out the clothespins from the newly washed diapers, and on and on. Once she was photographed holding a four-foot Mexican iguana, somewhat gingerly, but above all triumphantly. And once she shot a rattlesnake on the edge of the badminton court before a gallery of admiring boys. Her Eastern relatives and friends must have listened popeyed to her adventures in a West that sounded quite as wild and fearsome as they had hopefully imagined.

But not only Easterners think of the desert as a place filled with deadly animals of deadly intent; many Tucson residents are undoubtedly of the same opinion. Of all our animal neighbors the few so-called dangerous ones are among the most misunderstood. Many creatures, popularly believed to be dangerous, aren't so at all, such as the tarantula, the centipede, and most of the scorpions. If you live in the desert, it is important to know which ones you need to worry about, for people have actually died of fear from being bitten by a harmless animal they thought to be poisonous. Only five can normally be considered dangerous: the rattlesnake, the coral snake, the Gila monster, the slender bark, or rock, scorpion, and the black widow.

As I have said, Arizona is rich in rattlers, having seventeen different kinds. They come in all colors and sizes from the small mountain rattlers of eighteen inches to the five-or-six-foot diamondbacks. They occur at all elevations from sea level to ten thousand feet and they are both nocturnal and diurnal, depending on the temperature. For injecting the venom they enjoy a highly developed system of long, hollow, folding fangs that work on the same principle as the hypodermic needle. These are replaceable and, in fact, are periodically shed. Contrary to popular opinion, the mortality rate due to rattlesnake bite is only two to three per cent, more people being killed by lightning.

The rattlesnake is a viper and therefore ovoviviparous, meaning that the eggs hatch within the mother so that she gives birth to living young, a habit the vipers share with certain other snakes such as garter snakes, water snakes, and boas. Most of the rest are oviparous, the mother laying her eggs in a protected spot where they undergo incubation without further attention from her. Lizards also fall in either category, though mostly they lay eggs. All turtles are oviparous and we, being mammals, are viviparous.

More specifically the rattlesnake is a pit viper, meaning that he has a "pit" located between the eye and the nostril, which is sensitive to heat and aids him in directing his strike effectively at his warm-blooded prey. If you live in the desert, as we do, you occasionally find a rattlesnake in the vicinity, though many of our friends have never seen one except at the Museum. However, we find fewer around our house than does a friend who lives outside New York City.

One of the most common misconceptions about the rattlesnake is that he always rattles a warning before he strikes. Alas, he has no such gallant manners and merely vibrates his tail when he's nervous, as do many snakes. Sometimes a harmless gopher snake vibrating his tail in dry leaves will persuade the passerby into thinking he has heard a rattlesnake. Another misconception is that the number of rattles indicates the snake's age, but a rattlesnake acquires a new rattle each time he sheds his skin, which may be as many as five times a year.

The Arizona coral snake is quite a different kettle of snake from the southeastern species, being much smaller (seldom over twenty inches long) and of a usually gentle disposition. No instances of death due to this coral snake's bite have been recorded and almost no instances of a bite in which venom was injected. The venom can be presumed to be potent, since coral snakes belong to the same family as the cobra and most of this family have a dangerous neurotoxic venom. Like the cobra, the coral snake also has short, rigid fangs. It is generally nocturnal and lives on small snakes, its favorite food being the small worm, or blind, snake.

The trouble with the coral snake is that people have difficulty in identifying him. They tend to think that any snake is a coral snake which has red in its pattern, and the desert has many such. A simple sentence is supposed to solve the dilemma, at least here: the coral snake is the only snake that has red, whitish, and black bands, in that order, completely encircling the body. The shovel-nosed snake has the same color pattern but the red bands do not cross its white stomach and it does not have a solid black head as does the coral snake. It is very much of a mystery why so many of the nocturnal and burrowing snakes are brightly colored, for in the dark their brilliant patterns cannot be seen.

The Gila monster and its close relative, the Mexican beaded lizard, are the only two poisonous lizards in the world. They have a true poison secreted by glands in the lower jaw, rather than just a dirty mouth, as some people think. One of the most preposterous of the legends about the Gila monster is that he has no elimination, hence the reason for his being considered foul-mouthed. Although the venom is potent and can be compared to that of the rattlesnake, few if any deaths can be attributed entirely to the effects of Gila monster bite, presumably because of its inability to inject the venom. When a Gila monster bites he hangs on tightly with powerful jaws, as does any lizard, so the quicker he can be removed the better, though this may be difficult. My husband was once bitten by a Gila monster, which nipped him on the hand through the sack in which he was confined. He experienced some local swelling, considerable pain, and profuse bleeding.

This matter of a Gila monster's venom is an interesting one. Since his food consists largely of eggs and baby animals which he simply gulps down whole, he has no need of it and is probably unaware that he has it. Therefore there is some reason to believe that this secretion, as far as the Gila monster is concerned, is just an aid in digestion and that it is accidentally poisonous to mammals. Very rarely do we come upon a Gila monster in the wild; I have seen but one outside the Museum—he was crossing our driveway one summer evening. And the boys hardly ever report seeing one when they are out hiking. They can be thought of as a hazard only if touched or picked up, in which case they would properly bite you in self-defense. As they are protected in this state, you have no business picking one up anyway.

The slender bark, or rock, scorpion, which is the only one of the more than twenty species in Arizona that can be considered dangerous, is mainly so to very small children or people with a heart condition. Our nine-year-old, our eleven-year-old, and I have all been stung by this scorpion with no effect other than the characteristic tingling sensation of the afflicted part. Michael, who was stung on the stomach, complained for a while that his feet and hands felt as if they were asleep, but this wore off quickly. If a

A Gila monster, shown protected by natural camouflage

PHOTO BY AL MORGAN, ARIZONA-SONORA DESERT MUSEUM

scorpion sting leaves a swelling, it is not the dangerous kind. The reason for this is that the venom of the dangerous kind is neurotoxic and does not produce much of a local reaction. This fellow usually clings to the underside of objects, so when you turn over a stone or a board, it is wise to hold it by its edges. Application of a tourniquet for a short period and of ice for an hour or two is the recommended treatment for scorpion sting.

Sometimes we find a black widow in the boys' playhouse or among their toys in an outside cabinet, but it would be just as likely for my brother living in Philadelphia to find one in his children's playhouse, for the black widow is not unique to the desert and is probably commoner in other areas. It is very shy and retiring and will seldom bite unless injured. But the exception is

From left to right: giant hairy scorpion, striped-tail scorpion, and bark, or rock, scorpion (dangerous to small children)

PHOTO BY MERVIN W. LARSON, ARIZONA-SONORA DESERT MUSEUM

always waiting to pounce—that little bit of indeterminism that keeps the scientist cagey and the rest of us from being bored.

Once we were visiting one of Disney's photographers, whose specialty was close-ups of insects and spiders (in fact most of his house was given over to them, ants alone occupying the living room and dining room), and I was told to wiggle my finger above a certain black widow's web. The result of this action, which I performed with a pencil, was that the black widow popped out in a most menacing and atypical fashion. What titillated my husband was whether this aggressive behavior could be a genetic trait capable of being passed on to its offspring, an alarming prospect. A black widow's bite is extremely painful and can be dangerous, though the overall mortality rate is probably less than three per cent.

Bees and wasps kill more people yearly than do any of the traditionally dangerous animals because so many thousands of people are stung by them, a certain percentage of whom are allergic. Some people are also allergic to ant bites or stings (some ants bite and others sting). A friend of ours was bitten by a red ant while walking barefoot up to our house from the stream, and before reaching home she was almost in a coma. Our boys are bitten regularly by a variety of ants, usually on a toe, which becomes red, hot, and swollen. Ice water or ice packs seem to be as effective a treatment as any. In spite of his many ant bites (or stings), Hugh maintains a certain sympathy for them, and once when we were driving along after a heavy summer rain, he said commiseratingly, "To an ant this would be a dreadful flood, wouldn't it?"

Another troublesome insect is the blood-sucking conenose, a bug of many aliases such as kissing bug, assassin bug, and Walpai tiger. Like the mosquito it lives on blood, and its "bite", similar to that of the mosquito, customarily leaves only a red welt. However, some people, I being one, are very allergic to it, suffering severe cramps and nausea. This creature is parasitic to the wood rat or pack rat, and lives cosily with them in their nests. It emerges in the spring, being seen mostly in May and June, especially at night in one's house, for it is attracted by the light as well as by the prospect of a meal. To eliminate this creature one has to eliminate the pack-rat nests in the immediate area.

The centipede, like the tarantula, looks much worse than he is. For that he is needlessly blamed, and squashed. He can bite, this being painful but not serious, and his claws have no poison. If they should ever leave a series of red marks after crawling over you, as is so often heard, the only explanation is your abnormally sensitive skin and a centipede with dirty feet. The Arizona tarantula's bite is even less painful than that of a bee. I don't know why it is that *his* furriness should so revolt people who are always talking about nice little furry animals, which describes tarantulas perfectly. The same holds true for fuzzy caterpillars.

As far as the dangerousness of other animals such as the peccary and mountain lion is concerned, they are no different than

Western diamondback rattlesnake

PHOTO BY ELIZABETH T. WOODIN

any wild animal who will protect himself as best he can when cornered. The stories of the peccary's ferocity are wildly exaggerated and usually result from the animal becoming confused and rushing towards the person instead of away. Granted a fifty-pound boar dashing towards you, clicking his tusks, is not a sight to inspire calm, but nevertheless reason must prevail, and one must remember that the poor animal is simply scared and muddled.

Mountain lions have been known to follow people, but out of curiosity rather than with sinister intent. In the Huachuca Mountains to the southeast of here, a friend of ours was walking along one summer night looking for some bug or other by flashlight when suddenly he "felt" that he was being watched. The next morning he found large mountain lion pad-marks paralleling his previous night's excursion, which, far from alarming him, delighted him. Having spent so many years scrutinizing with fascination other forms of fauna, he liked the idea that one of them at last was returning the attention.

6

The Mountain

MOUNTAINS, forever rimming man's horizon, are a focus to his wandering eye, a lodestar to his wandering heart. Come to me, they softly say, and I will reveal to you, only to you, my shadowed secrets and airy exultation. Entranced, the feet move upwards. But I wonder if the enchantment of mountains is not due partly to the fact that from their heights we can look down on our fellows and shout, "I'm the King of the Castle and you're the Dirty Rascal."

In many ways the desert mountains are more tantalizing than others. Rising high out of the heat and sand, their crests darkened by trees, they suggest a different and more congenial world. The oven-heat of a desert summer is not so unbearable if you know that with a car and an hour you can be in sweater weather. Then the mountains become a refuge, offering the sound of wind in pine tops, the smell of sun on pine needles, and cool shadows. In the winter they offer snow and icicles to the curious and nostalgic, skiing to the sportsman.

To the naturalist the desert mountains are an endlessly fascinating field of study. As one proceeds up their stony slopes not only does the temperature decrease, but the rainfall increases; sometimes a yearly difference of as much as twenty inches existing between the base and the summit. This changing climate naturally produces flora and fauna quite unlike those of the surrounding desert. More specifically each mountain is a pyramid of life zones characterized by distinctive plant and animal life, though the edges of these are by no means sharply defined. Our Arizona mountains are an excellent example of this life-zone situation, illustrating changes that otherwise can be found only by traveling from here to northern Canada. Even to the layman the gradual vegetative transformation achieved by driving from Tucson to the top of the nearby Catalinas is visually noticeable and exciting.

On leaving the city we first go through the creosote desert where round-tailed ground squirrels and rabbits burrow happily in the fine-textured soil and scurry around, careful to keep out of the way of hungry diamondback and Mojave rattlesnakes. Briefly we dip down into several mesquite-filled creek bottoms before winding up through the foothills, in whose more varied and abundant growth the black-throated sparrow prefers to nest. Palo verde, ocotillo, brittle-bush, saguaros, and several of the smaller cacti flourish here, along with the Harris ground squirrel, the tiger rattlesnake, and the usual complement of rabbits.

This phase of the Lower Sonoran life zone spreads onto the mountain itself, stretching up to an altitude of approximately four thousand feet, where it gives way to a narrow band of desert grassland dotted with agaves. As we proceed higher we pass through an open woodland of spreading evergreen oaks and yuccas, the breeding ground of the bridled titmouse. Gradually the growth becomes dense as manzanita, juniper, other oaks, and the piñon pine infiltrate. Here we stop for a picnic lunch which we share with the Steller's jays who come to scold but stay to eat, and the boys scout about in hopes of finding a mountain kingsnake, a black-tailed rattler, or a porcupine. Off again, we climb up above seven thousand feet and into the ponderosa pine forests which replace the oaks. If we are lucky we will see crossing the road a striped skunk, or a glossy black rattlesnake with yellow bars, or even a bear. As we near the mountain top, the north slopes are forested with Douglas firs, trees several hundred years old and up to four or five feet in diameter. If we knew where to look we could discover the nests of the hermit thrush and red-breasted nuthatch. And then, above this, at nine thousand feet, we could walk under alpine fir that typify the Hudsonian zone of northern Canada, and watch golden-crowned kinglets flutter in the treetops after insects.

The various bird groupings are particularly noteworthy because they locate themselves according to the appearance or growth-form of the vegetation. A mountain chickadee is prepared to catch the insects that he likes to eat in needle trees, whereas the bridled titmouse hunts for the same kind of insects in evergreen oaks; and neither bird can successfully find its prey in the other's trees, a very sensible arrangement.

Another aspect that interests the scientist in our desert mountains is the slight but observable differences displayed by certain animal populations of various ranges. Thousands of years ago when the climate grew warmer, the animals who did not like the heat moved up into the mountains. On these islands surrounded by a desert sea, they were as effectively isolated as though surrounded by actual water, a perfect setting in which speciation can occur, for when the differences between two groups of the same kind of animal become consistent and sufficiently marked, then the animals are considered as separate races or even species.

The phenomenon of speciation due to isolation and selection is most dramatically illustrated in the Galápagos Islands where, because of it, Darwin received the impetus to a line of thought that culminated in the *Origin of Species*. Darwin noticed the wide variation among divers kinds of animals. Not only were many of the plant and animal species different from those on the mainland, but they varied significantly among the islands of the archipelago itself. Evolution in a nutshell. The large, lumbering, land tortoise, confined to the island on which he was born, is an excellent example of this. First of all, he is a far cry from his present cousins on the mainland, growing to the impressive length of four feet (I once sat on one and he carried me off piggyback as if I were a fly), and secondly, he has his reproducible differences from island to island.

The Galápagos finches are another example, perhaps more notable to the layman for their remarkable adaptation to the island conditions than for any variances from island to island. After their arrival in the islands they filled the available ecological niches usually occupied by other kinds of birds that here were absent. Some kept the typical thick beak of the seed-eating finches, some evolved the warblerlike beak of the insect-eating birds, some the long beak of the flower-probing birds, some the rather parrot-like beak of the leaf- and fruit-eating birds, and some the wood-peckerlike beak of the wood-boring birds. Among this latter group one ingenious species further resembles a woodpecker by climbing up and down branches and trunks in a most unfinchlike fashion, but most astonishing of all, he substitutes for the woodpecker's long tongue a twig that he holds lengthwise in his bill. With this he pokes into a crack or hole to force out the insect, which he promptly grabs.

To bring things closer to home, the mountain kingsnake or coral kingsnake, a harmless and colorful creature of alternating black, red, and white bands, varies in both pattern and scalation among certain mountain ranges, a fact that so interested my husband that he chose this snake as the subject of his master's thesis: "Ecology and Geographic Variation of the Arizona Mountain Kingsnake." He jokingly said he was in a quandary, for the particular subspecies inhabiting the Huachuca Mountains of southeastern Arizona had been named after him: *Lampropeltis pyromelana woodini*. Should his investigations end by showing that this race was not different enough to warrant its being classed separately, then he would be robbing himself of his claim to immortality. And how many of one's friends have a snake named after them?

In order to accumulate the necessary data for this thesis we spent our third married summer in a remote cabin perched high up one of the cool canyons of the Huachuca Mountains. There, lounging in a chair in the shade of a spreading live oak, our first-born eating grass beside me, I abounded with that distinct smugness ascribed to kings in their castles as I viewed the baking valley floor far below, shimmering in the August heat. Behind me rose the cracked pink canyon walls and above them hovered the bluish mountains. The gazing eye wavered helplessly back and forth between them, caught in a tension of opposing beauty.

The business of "collecting" up to this time had been more or less a mystery to me and one that I was still content to leave unexplored. For the first few mornings I watched my husband set off with a snake bag or two tied to his belt, a small pick in one hand and forceps for picking up rock rattlers in a back pocket. And I watched him return in the late afternoon with at least one prize and sometimes more. What went on between his departure and return soon began to tease my imagination uncontrollably, so one day I asked, "What do you do in the mountains?"

"I just poke around here and there, turning over rotten logs and things." And I had a lovely vision of him ambling along up the canyon with the sunlight filtering through the leaves of the maples and occasional glimpses of high cliffs or pine-clad mountain peaks, the birds singing, squirrels chattering, the rabbits scuttling. Then a snake would slither into the picture and spoil it. Apparently kingsnakes were usually to be found in the canyon bottom, black-tailed rattlers almost anywhere, and the small rock rattlers in the south-facing rock slides. These latter could be discovered by throwing rocks about in the slide and then waiting for the telltale rattle. That summer Bill caught over two dozen in this way, a system so dependable that you could announce at the breakfast table, "Well, I think I'll go catch me a rock rattler!" and be back in an hour with one if not two.

Later, he showed me how I was to catch a snake should I see one, and afterwards, whenever I returned from a sunny afternoon stroll, he would greet me with "Catch any snakes, dear?" This

Peter and I

meant exactly the same thing as "See any snakes, dear?", for a seen snake ought to be a caught snake. This query never hinted at any levity or idle curiosity. I once made the mistake of answering "No, but I saw a kingsnake wriggle into a hole in the stone wall." Suffice it to say that back-packing a year-old child is not a legitimate excuse for shirking one's duty. Strangely enough I never saw another snake. In fact, I manage never to see a snake in the wild unless it has first been seen by my husband.

The Huachuca Mountains are a naturalist's paradise. Stretching across the border into Mexico, they form a land bridge for various kinds of wildlife that appear in the United States only at this point. The mountains that summer were teeming with determined scientists in eager pursuit of rare zoological specimens. It was impossible to enjoy a peaceful walk through the mountains without stumbling on a bat-man or a bug-man or an ant-man or a bird-man or my snake-man, each armed with the accouterments of his trade, slinking along after some creature hidden behind leaf or log. Often Bill would appear for dinner with one of these gentlemen in tow and the evening would be enlivened with tales of their respective exploits.

Determined not to be left behind all of the time, I stuffed our year-old son Peter into an old army knapsack in which I had cut two holes for his legs, and with him on my back we took off after my husband. Some sleek New York tourists once came upon the three of us as we were crossing the road below our cabin. Bill had a three-day beard, a well-ventilated T-shirt, and ragged pants; I was in patched blue jeans, hair in pigtails, and my toes sticking out of my sneakers; Peter was crowing happily on my back, munching on a cracker and in a state which can only be described as grubby. The long black Cadillac stopped, a white-gloved hand rolled down a window, and a delicate silvery voice asked in the most polite and winning tones if we would object to having our pictures taken. We silently assented with curt nods of the head and stood at rigid attention looking fiercely into the camera lens. After the click we turned on our heels and strode haughtily away, I five dutiful paces behind my husband. We realized that on our shoulders rested the reputation of the wild Mountain Folk.

I learned an enormous amount that summer. I learned how to pick up ants, the difference between those that bite and those that sting, how to tell a black-chinned hummingbird from a Costa's, how to identify a trogon, where to find bats in the daytime and how to be a midwife to a horned toad (really a lizard). The expectant mother awaited her time at the bottom of a gallon jar and started to produce her young one morning while I was in the midst of dusting. Before I was through she had presented me with thirty babies. Each tiny lizard was tightly curled in its own transparent sack. "Ovoviviparous," I said to myself, "definitely ovoviviparous." With a vigorous wriggle they would free themselves, dart off, and partly bury themselves in the sand. Characteristically, Mama paid not the slightest attention to her offspring at any time.

They were unbelievably small, not much more than an inch long, and startlingly like their parents in every detail, even to the prickly tail and minute horns crowning their heads. Theirs was the charm of the miniature, and, entranced, I held one in my hand for a long time. I was about to return it to its brothers and sisters when I remembered that admiration by itself is scientifically unproductive. Not wishing to neglect my responsibilities, I searched my mind for some appropriate task that I could perform. Having observed that sooner or later scientists measure, I went to find a ruler and on this I painstakingly placed each of the thirty newborns in turn, duly noting down the results on my grocery pad. This took me the rest of the morning, and when my husband

A horned lizard, the common local species of horned "toad"

returned for lunch I presented him with a long list of figures in place of the expected blueberry muffins. Man shall not live by bread alone.

As a reward for my industry Bill took Peter and me along when he went to collect in a neighboring canyon, choosing for us an enchanted place called "the box" in which to spend the hours that he was off in search of reptiles. There the canyon walls drew close together, forming a long narrow cleft a hundred feet or more in length and perhaps ten feet in width. The walls towered straight overhead, and between them ran a stream. A short way beyond the upper end of the box one climbed, by dint of some effort, over a huge pile of driftwood wedged between one canyon wall and a sycamore that blocked the entrance, into a tiny oval spot, room-sized and bewitched. It was a secret verdant pocket

> Where oxslips and the nodding violet grows
> Quite over-canopied with luscious woodbine,
> With sweet musk-roses and with eglantine:
> There sleeps Titania some time of the night,
> Lull'd in these flowers with dances and delight;
> And there the snake throws her enamell'd skin,
> Weed wide enough to wrap a fairy in.

Only here the oxslips were yellow columbine, the violets bright red penstemon, and the canopy of sunlighted sycamore leaves. We were enclosed by evergreen-edged canyon walls that were high enough to protect but not so high as to smother. Upstream the water came pouring in over a boulder, spreading out over its mossy surface in a lace-fan waterfall, until it fell into the dark pool, where it stirred up bubbles and froth. Downstream it ran out over the driftwood pile to disappear below.

The furniture was small, uncrowded, and quite in keeping: two maple saplings leaning out from one wall, a few shrubs from the other, a grassy bank, a pool, bunches of flowers, and maidenhair ferns sprouting from crevices. Overhead shone a silver thread where a spider glided. Beyond it the fingered leaves of

"The Box" in Ramsay Canyon of the Huachuca Mountains

the sycamore patterned the blue sky-patch across which a buzzard would briefly sail. The bubbling water and the occasional hoyden screech of a jay were the only sounds. Elfin folk must have lived there as surely as in an Irish wood, hospitable ones I thought, for Peter and I spent the day unmolested, an Hyblean day between two waterfalls.

Peter, the changeling child, caught water beetles, paddled in the pool, and sat on a rock singing, with a snail in one hand and the fingers of the other dipping into the water to throw silver beads at the dragonflies come to play. Then a new-seen daddy-long-legs confronted his astonished eyes, and he laughed as it crawled over his bare leg. Beside him grew a clump of horsetails, or scouring rushes, reeds like bamboo that are one of the most ancient plants still growing. They flourished in the carboniferous age long before the time of the dinosaurs. Alas, I did not know how to make them into Pan-pipes with which to lure out the hidden sprites. So I leaned against the sycamore instead and briefly

"Titania's Pool" in Ramsay Canyon

watched an ant drag away a fallen comrade for who knows what purpose, watched a butterfly drift by like a flake of sunshine, watched the shadows flicker over the pool and the few fingers of sunlight move along the bottom, illuminating each suspended particle of sand. Then my eyes caught on the blue mountain peaks just visible in the cleft through which the stream came. There they stayed, remembering other mountain peaks that similarly ensnared my eyes, snow-covered ones with ice-blue shadows. I tended them one afternoon, leaning against an aspen whose golden leaves trembled with such an intensity of light against the sky that my impaled senses also trembled. As long as I sat still enough the beat within me was echoed then also in the butterfly opening and shutting its wings, in the warm bark of the tree at my back, in the earth, in the high peaks, in the light, most of all in the light. And then also I felt under my fingers the essence of all things: the hardness of the rock, the smoothness of a leaf, the warmth of the sun.

I remembered, almost with anguish, that long-gone afternoon when beauty first squeezed my soul. It happened when I stood up to leave; the beauty suddenly expanded, became more radiant, and soared away from me. Then I thought myself to be outside, detached from its immortal flow, and I felt such a terrible helplessness, such a yearning to possess it, that, being young and self-conscious, I wished for a camera as another might have wished for a pencil or a paintbrush, because I could not bear its transiency. Not until our Huachuca summer, living as we did in the lap of a beautiful mountain, did I learn that the only place to keep such things is behind the eyes in the magic lantern of the mind. Now I set those moments adrift in my memory, where they float like glass beads in an ocean. When I wish, I go afishing, cast forth my net to catch them, and then I choose one and hold it in the palm of my hand all wet and shining.

So the mountains benevolently endowed the summer with moments of bliss as well as with reptiles. Peter and I kept cool, and Bill gathered the creatures that so delighted him until the cabin bulged with specimens in jars, bags, and boxes. The more treasured of the harmless snakes were kept in bags in a corner of the living room, but from there the bags were apt to wander. One evening we had some callers, a charming elderly couple who wanted to be neighborly.

"And so you collect snakes. How interesting!" the old gentleman said brightly to my husband.

"Yes, isn't it," voiced I. "And he's been after them since babyhood, poor things."

"Really! His poor mother!" said the lady. And to me, "And you, my dear. Do you *like* those snakes?" She shuddered delicately.

"I don't mind them if they're in cages."

"It is safe—with the baby, I mean. But then I know you must keep them far away from him."

Peter, who had been staring unblinkingly at our visitors, crawled off to the "snake corner" and was patting and poking one of the sacks. Each time the contents wiggled, he gave an enraptured squeal.

"Peter!" sternly said his father as he went over to him, removed the sack from his hands, and put him in the playpen. "No, no, don't touch! You'll hurt them!"

"Are there snakes in those bags?" asked the lady.

"Yes, we keep them in here so they won't get too hot." And my husband went on to explain the reptilian lack of thermostatic equipment, but the lady wasn't listening. Righteous indignation oozing from every pore, she gasped, "Men like you shouldn't *have* children," looking over at Peter as though she were about to snatch him away. By this time the old gentleman was muttering to Bill in an undertone something about not paying any attention to hysterical women. Three of the sacks chose this auspicious moment to lurch out of their corner and begin to writhe and dance, casting strange, contorted shadows on the wall behind them.

"Oh, oh!" said the lady, catching sight of them. "Oh, no!" She sprang to her feet, rushed to her husband's side and all in a rush poured out the ingrained polite civilities of a departing guest before disappearing into the night, dragging her husband behind her.

Three days later I almost stepped on a black-tailed rattlesnake that was sunning himself on the path. I was convinced it was one of the twenty-two Bill kept in the shed, so until his return I bolted myself and Peter in the cabin, certain that we were surrounded by hordes of escaped and vengeful rattlers. Then it was that I wondered if that lady didn't have a legitimate point of view after all, and that this snake business was really for the birds.

Another time I complained one morning that the mice in the kitchen were becoming impossible, leaving their droppings all over the dishes and chewing holes in the packaged foods.

"I have just the thing, a guaranteed cure for your mouse troubles," said Bill, going out to the porch. While waiting for him to come back I thought how clever he was to have anticipated this emergency and to have brought along some mousetraps. A few minutes later he returned with a large gopher snake in each hand. Before I could utter a word of protest he had turned them loose down the hole by the stove.

For the rest of the summer I lived in dread of suddenly coming upon the snakes in some out-of-the-way nook in the kitchen. It was bad enough to open the icebox for the breakfast bacon and be met by the glassy stare of a frozen lizard, or to approach the sink only to find it filled with preserved snakes soaking in water.

One day we were taken to an old abandoned well "chuck full of them snakes," said our guide. Usually such tales turn out rather differently than the flowery introductory remarks would lead one to expect, and the masses of snakes on inspection turn out to be two or three at the most. Much to Bill's surprise, and my apprehension, we saw, when we peered down into the shallow dry well, over a dozen snakes of different species in a frightening tangle at the bottom. Some must have been trapped there a long time, for they were exceedingly scrawny. A ladder was placed into the well so that Bill could reach them, and his reappearance with two fist-fuls of writhing snakes was quite as fearful a sight as that of Perseus with the head of Medusa, and almost as calamitous, for I was convinced I was about to share the fate of Polydectes and, in my fright, be turned to stone.

But snakes were by no means the only form of wildlife to which I was closely exposed that summer. Bill came home one afternoon with a little brown furry animal at the bottom of his snake bag.

"Well, what do you think it is?" he asked, holding it out to me on the palm of his hand. It had a long, faintly ringed tail, long digging claws, a long thin snout that turned up at the end, small neat round ears, and a masked face reminiscent of a coon. I had to admit that I could not even concoct a guess.

"It's a coatimundi, though locally he is known as 'chulo.' I found him half-dead and lying in the middle of the trail covered with ants. Must have been deserted by his family. Cute little devil, isn't he?" At this bit of flattery the strange animal roused himself from the middle of Bill's hand and looked around, twitching his nose ever so slightly. Bill set him on the floor and he went ambling off to explore, with a rolling nautical gait. He was about five inches long with another five inches of tail that he usually held perpendicular. As I soon learned, he was enormously, even tryingly, mischievous, and very little if anything escaped his beady black eyes.

As I had not dared to confess that I hadn't the remotest idea what a coatimundi was, I surreptitiously looked him up in our reference book and learned that this creature, belonging to the same family as the raccoon, came up from Mexico to barely range into Arizona. (In recent years these have extended their range northward.) He was omnivorous, eating, among other things, fruit, young birds, lizards, and insects.

Some of the items on the gastronomic list I found disturbing, but enthralled by the immediate charm of that small animal, I dismissed from my mind any qualms as to what my role as adopted

Chulo, the baby coatimundi

parent might involve. We were later told of bands of over fifty being seen in these mountains, traveling quickly and agilely on the ground and through the trees like monkeys, chittering and squeaking to each other. They also have the reputation of being death on dogs, able to disembowel them in short order with their long canine teeth.

Throughout the summer Chulo proved a most engaging pet. He throve on the same diet as Peter, mostly milk, fruit, and vitamins, and the two became great friends. An old classmate of Bill's, who stopped by on his way home from Europe, was incredulous when he first saw Peter and Chulo sitting side by side in the playpen. With a great deal of satisfaction I was able to explain what kind of creature each was. He professed more amazement at the wild one than at the domestic one, but I think each came in for a fair share of his interest, as my husband was the first of his school class to succumb to fatherhood. I can think of few more confusing experiences of youth than that of coming for the first time upon a childhood friend with a child of his own, when one is still childless oneself. Logically it follows all the laws one has been taught and accepts, but emotionally it is bewildering. Once more we are reminded that we indeed go the way of all flesh.

We also had a ghost in our mountain retreat. The cabin had been built many years ago by a Dr. Biedermann, a remarkable and scholarly man who came to these mountains at the turn of the century because he was interested in the flora and fauna of the area. His thorough and meticulous observations for the Smithsonian Institution were of tremendous value and greatly added to the zoological and botanical knowledge of the time. He had also been, we were told, a cousin of Schubert and one of Lincoln's bodyguards. He lived in the Huachucas until he died and was buried several hundred feet beyond the cabin.

We were sometimes awakened at night by a slow heavy tread, like footsteps across our tin roof. "Dr. Biedermann!" I would whisper nervously from beneath the covers. "Humph!" my husband would answer, and though he would not admit to a ghost, he never could explain the measured tread. Later we heard someone attribute such sounds to coons. But how can coons manage to sound like a large heavy man walking slowly across your roof?

Chulo   *Chulo and Peter*

Sitting alone at night while Bill was off driving the valley roads in search of nocturnal snakes, I found Dr. Biedermann's periodic wanderings uncomfortably close no matter how enthusiastically I might countenance them, even plead for them, during the day. The wind would whine down the canyon and scrape the branches of the overhanging oak tree against the roof. Moon shadows, set in motion by the wind, would come through the window and quiver on the floor until a cloud blotted them out. And always there were the silent undulations of the snake bags.

By the light of a smoking kerosene lamp we celebrated our second anniversary. In the middle of the unsteady table on the porch a few scarlet penstemons in a jam jar stirred in the careless evening breeze that stole down so cool from the mountain tops. Our son was asleep, the canyon was darkening, as was the valley below, and the moon-sliver rocked in and out of the clouds. It was quiet and it was silent. In front of each of us was an almost cold glass of champagne and a steak cooked on the week's trash fire. As I watched my husband, who was somewhat abstractedly (he was undoubtedly musing on what prizes tomorrow would bring) and yet contentedly chewing his steak, I wouldn't have changed that porch for Ondine's, nor for the Pavillon, nor hardly at all for Lasserre or Florian's.

The summer drew to a close; I hated to see it slip by. Each day slid down the throat of summer as easily as the ripe peaches slid down ours. In the regular procession of sparkling days, in our human isolation and deep-felt accord with ourselves as a family, as well as with the mountains in which we lived, we enjoyed a kind of magic. And loneliness was a word that held no meaning. I think of ourselves then as remote and undefinable. Wrapped in the time-lessness of the mountains, we had lost our identity and became anonymous, generic. We were the Man, the Woman, the Child, living with the Mountain. During the day I heard it sigh, at night I felt its heart throb, and I wondered if our canyon were not en-chanted and we its happy captives.

PHOTO BY TAD NICHOLS

Glen Canyon, Colorado River, in 1955. The waters of Lake Powell, formed by the building of Glen Canyon Dam in the sixties, had covered two-thirds of the formation shown above by 1984.

7

The River

O F all the many marvels present in the desert, none is more startling to me than a river. Evanescent streams and dry washes are quite in character, but not a deep, wide river flowing, as it must, through rock and cactus-covered sand, roaring or whispering according to its fancy. It's such a simple thing, a river, merely a moving collection of water particles, but in a land as dry and motionless as ours it fascinates us inordinately. Therefore no prospect could be more appealing than that of floating down the Colorado through the northern desert. Add to this the respectable reason of scientific research and we're off.

In the fall of 1957 we joined a group of scientists who were planning to drift leisurely through Glen Canyon investigating their respective fields, for on completion of the dam above Lee's Ferry this canyon would be flooded, inundating not only some of the world's most spectacular scenery, but also many prehistoric Indian ruins and relics. This would be one of the last opportunities to see and study what would later be destroyed.

So it was that I found myself one evening in September in front of a small, waterproof, zipper bag, allotted to each member for his personal belongings, with the problem of packing into it the proper clothes for ten days on a river. I decided, after some deliberation, that—besides a camera, a large sun hat, and a sweater —two shorts, two shirts, two pairs of socks and a bar of strong brown laundry soap should outwardly see me through. As I was zipping up my bag, I happened to glance across the room to a growing mound of boxes and bags that my husband was busily assembling. At my indignant outburst he blandly explained, "But it's all my collecting equipment!" What men have been allowed to get away with through the centuries in the name of science!

Besides the boatmen and the invaluable wives who were going to cook, the expedition consisted of an anthropologist, a botanist, a geologist, an ornithologist, a herpetologist (my husband), and a doctor. The latter, to me, was of the greatest importance, for I am too much the product of civilization to be entirely comfortable in inaccessible places without medical aid at hand. The idea of an appendectomy performed with a penknife, by someone who many years ago may have received an A in Biology for dissecting a frog, fills me with nothing but horror.

Our starting point was a small dot on the map, Hite, Utah; and our destination an equally small dot about 170 miles downstream on the Colorado, Lee's Ferry, Arizona. To get to the beginning and have our car waiting for us at the end involved leaving our car at the end and flying to the beginning. Early one morning we stood in the middle of nowhere beside a pole from which hung a limp yellow wind-sock. All around us stretched a vast and silent desert. Then from behind a cliff appeared a silver dot that slowly grew into a plane, which landed and taxied up to us.

We piled our respective zipper bags, the mound of collecting equipment, and ourselves into this flying flea and off we flew to Hite. Beneath us smoothly slipped an incredibly rough desert of sandstone mesas, upthrust mountains, and deep narrow canyons that wriggled like serpents down to the Colorado. In the middle of this desolation and oblivious to it, the big river had carved itself a long and glorious house called the Glen Canyon. Its sheltering red walls tower close to two thousand feet, and between them the river flows placidly onward with no memory of its wild turbulence to the north and no thought of its wilder turbulence to come.

Until the building of the new dam, the 150-mile-long canyon showed no wounds from the hand of man. The first white men to venture across it were a group of Spanish explorers led by two Franciscan friars, Domínguez and Escalante, in the middle 1770's. In the following century occasional trappers and traders penetrated this wilderness, then Mormons, and finally the gold miners. At Lee's Ferry, which marks the end of Glen Canyon and the beginning of Marble Canyon, a hardy Mormon maintained a regular ferry service from 1873 on, and it remained in operation until the late 1920's when the bridge was built.

Once airborne, I am always on the lookout for a possible landing spot should disaster strike. Nothing could have been less comforting than the terrible jumble below us, a seething ocean of rock that had been lashed into a maelstrom by some violent and incomprehensible prehistoric wind. That we should be soon traversing it in a boat on a river seemed equally mad. What if the boat should spring an irreparable leak, what then? Even to my novitiate's eye the desert below seemed an impassable barrier, and in my apprehension I remembered a remark once made about this country. "Why friend, even a crow has to pack a canteen to fly over that godforsaken land!"

Assiduously I studied the geological map of the area spread out on my lap, and the magic of such phrases as the Kaiparowits Downwarp and the Waterpocket Monocline dispelled my gloomy thoughts and evoked an unrecognizable and mysterious world, until suddenly the river was again below us. The plane banked steeply, slipped in between the high canyon walls, and landed on a strip along the bank. After that maneuver even the prospect of having to hike back to civilization was immeasurably more pleasant than that of having to leave the way we had just arrived.

Except for the cleared runway, there was no sign that anyone had ever been here or ever intended to come. With our possessions piled around us, we watched the plane fly out of the canyon, leaving us to what we were sure was to be eternal soli-

tude. But before long, out of the silence and the sun, lurched a
noisy jeep to carry us to where the rest of the party were loading
the boats at the river's edge.

Hite consisted of a ferry crossing and a river check-station
where an attendant measured the amount and velocity of the water flowing by. The ferry was the typical kind of euphemism indig-
enous to out-of-the-way places, for it was merely a derelict craft
that spent most of its time stuck on a sand bar.

By midafternoon we were off, loaded into several San Juan
boats, which are eighteen-foot double-enders with decked-over
bow and stern, of extremely sturdy construction enabling them
to withstand a tremendous amount of pounding by water and
rocks. We were off, drifting on a brown ribbon of a river that,
century after century, had worn its slow persistent way down between its banks until now those banks were cliffs hanging above
our heads. As we slid under the footbridge, the checker had just
finished his calculations and he shouted down to us that we had
6750 second-feet of water, meaning that 6750 cubic feet of water
were passing a given point each second. It was hard to believe
that a little over two months before, there had been almost
100,000 cubic feet per second, but this marked fluctuation is typical of desert rivers.

As we were to be almost literally incarcerated in rock
for the duration of the trip, geology was undoubtedly the most
obvious aspect of it. Glen Canyon, through which we would be
traveling, is the type locality for certain of the lower Jurassic formations, these rock layers being known as the Glen Canyon
Group. At Hite, though, we found ourselves surrounded by
much older rock. At the river's edge was a grayish-tan layer of
Permian limestone, once the bottom of a Paleozoic sea laid down
over two hundred million years ago during what is called the age
of the amphibians. I amused myself that first hour by contemplating the terrible creatures that must have swum around in those
ancient waters, relieved that they were long gone, for I did not

wish them in the water through which my feet were trailing. It is a peculiar feeling to be shut in by walls that used to be the bottom of a primeval ocean.

Above this limestone were the three Triassic formations made when crocodile-like creatures roamed the earth, the most conspicuous of these being the Chinle, once a river or lake's flood plain. This looks like purple-gray sand dunes and it stands out in marked contrast to its neighboring formations. It is easily recognizable even to a layman's eye, especially in the Painted Desert to the southeast. In it one can sometimes find petrified logs and fossils. Above the Chinle, fifty million or so years later, comes the Glen Canyon Group marking the rise of the dinosaurs. The first of this group is the Wingate sandstone. As the afternoon wore on, it was the most prominent stratum, a great red wall on either side of us.

Normally, as one goes downstream and the river cuts deeper through the earth's surface, one would obviously progress to older and older formations. But here the strata had been so drastically tilted that instead we were going down to younger and younger rock. Once this confusing fact had finally penetrated my mind, I was able to make more sense out of what was passing by.

Around the campfire that night our anthropologist gave us two thousand years of Indian history in twenty minutes so that we would at least have some vague understanding of the ruins we would be seeing. The Indians who once lived in the Glen Canyon area belonged to a tribe called the Anasazi, appearing here shortly after the birth of Christ. At that time they were mostly sedentary, living in the open on sand banks, sheltering under crude brush ramadas or natural rock overhangs, or building pit houses of posts, sticks, and grass covered with dirt. They hunted, raised corn, and made baskets and unfired clay pots, a level of culture labeled Basketmaker by the archeologist. Later, when the bow and arrow and fired pottery had been added to their possessions, they become known as Modified Basketmaker.

Around the time of the Norman Conquest their culture was characterized by decorated fired pottery, a more formalized architecture using masonry, and a rather complex social structure. During the next two centuries more people utilized the area of the Glen Canyon, moving seasonally back and forth between it and the uplands, which was the cultural center. A desert river, offering water and arable flood plains, is bound to attract. However, in contrast to the Mississippi valley for example, the available land here was limited, owing to the river's channel taking up considerable space between the canyon walls.

Between A.D. 1100 and 1250 was the period of maximum utilization of the Glen Canyon basin by the Anasazi. After 1200 a pattern of movement to elevated ground and "urban" centers can be discerned. Reasons for these population shifts and abandonments is not known, though certain plausible ideas have been advanced, such as erosion of farmlands and increasing aridity, with possibly less moisture falling during the winter, which would affect the vital spring planting. Other explanations include intertribal war, nomadic raiders, plague, famine—the same old story. By A.D. 1300 this area was essentially abandoned by the Anasazi, and today it is very sparsely populated by a few Navajos, Paiutes, and Anglo ranchers.

Our first stop on the second day was at the mouth of Red Canyon, where stands an old cabin in which lived for a time a prospector by the name of Bert Loper, the "Grand Old Man of the Colorado." He spent much of his life on or beside the river and was killed just before his eightieth birthday on Mile 24½ Rapid of the Grand Canyon. On top of a nearby hill was our first Anasazi Indian ruin which our anthropologist dated at around A. D. 1100-1200. With eyes glued to the ground we scouted about for pieces of pottery and arrowheads as a source of possible added information on the ruin.

Later we came across some of their remarkably well preserved petroglyphs, or crude pictures picked or scratched into

Prehistoric Indian petroglyphs in Glen Canyon

the rock. Whether stylistic or naturalistic, they are mostly an undecipherable conglomeration, this particular one depicting more or less some sheep, short wavy lines like snakes, longer wavy lines that could possibly represent trails, a number of bare, very flat feet with minute toes, and strange triangular-shaped humans with stick arms and legs. Trying to interpet these creations would make a most interesting parlor game, judging from the wild samples produced that afternoon. I am always confusing

Drifting through Glen Canyon along cliffs of Navajo sandstone

petroglyphs with pictographs, and so I made use a useful jingle which I muttered to myself: "Petroglyphs are picked and pictographs are painted, a necessary fact with which to be acquainted."

The glaring sunlight, trapped in the canyon and shimmering off the cliffs and water, soon brought forth an astounding variety of sun hats and produced a prodigious thirst. We paused briefly to refill our canteens at the clear unmuddied spring called Dead Man Spring because several years ago our boatman came upon a corpse beside it. He later found out that the man had drowned six weeks before, ninety miles upstream on the Green. This is an example of the typical lore that makes the Colorado so very colorful to the ear as well as to the eye.

Over the lake, stream, and land deposits of the Wingate soon appeared the Navajo formation, once desert dunes that time had turned into sandstone. Ages later the river had sliced through them and left standing these mighty perpendicular cliffs whose pinkish-red surfaces are now stained with long dark streaks called "desert varnish," caused by the interaction of rain and iron within the rock, a sort of rust. These cliffs made me think of gigantic corroding hulls in dry dock.

Even a novice such as I could not mistake the Wingate for the Navajo. The former was not only darker in color but it weathered differently, its surface being angular, cracked, and uneven. Under the relentless wearing of the elements great chunks had broken off, leaving clean sharp edges. The Navajo, on the other hand, eroded into cones and domes, into caves and alcoves, into soft curves and arches, the most famous of which is Rainbow Bridge.

As the afternoon dwindled we stopped for the night at the foot of Tapestry Wall, a magnificent vast expanse of streaked Navajo sandstone three-quarters of a mile long and just under a thousand feet high, though to my unpracticed eye it looked longer and far higher. A heavy dew was falling when we turned in, so we buried ourselves in our sleeping bags, with the stars not farther than the canyon's rim and no sound but that of the whispering river and the wind as they passed to another world.

We awoke to find ourselves in the midst of a dust storm. Sand was in our hair, in our eyes; it had sifted into our beds and coated our skin; and we ate it for breakfast. The wind was blowing up river, kicking up choppy little waves, so our progress was slow and wet. Those in the bows, after the second or third cold dousing, had retreated behind tarps.

We landed at Olympic Bar to see the remains of a small gold-mining operation. The gold rush, in search of placer gold to be found in the gravels along the river banks, was launched in the early 1880's and brought to this area several hundred intrepid prospectors whose workings briefly clung to the canyon walls up and down the river. More recently it was uranium hunters who hammered in their stakes. Here the remains of an ingenious water wheel hung over the river, once adjustable to the everchanging water level. It had pumped water up to a storage tank at the top of a hill and from there the water had run down through a sluice to wash the gravel.

Under a board Bill found his first specimen, a spotted night snake, which, being a hard-to-find nocturnal species, pleased him. The rest of us picked up bright pebbles of jasper and agate. Whenever we stepped ashore, even we laymen scurried off with heads bent scrutinizing the ground at our feet, for the surrounding scientific flurry was catching, and one must make at least a pretense of searching for something. Then it is that the alchemy occurs and the world is transformed into something different, for knowledge has begun to illuminate its mysterious poetry.

Worn into the sandy bank where we stopped for lunch was a beaver slide. I had been feeling sorry for the beaver with not enough trees around out of which to make dams and houses, but Bill informed me that these beavers had adapted themselves to desert conditions so well that they were content to live in holes in the banks and to give up dam building. At this spot the canyon wall had withdrawn, leaving a flat plain dotted with small oak groves. Under one of these trees I found a perfect juvenile beaver skull which I took home to the boys. Cottonwoods grew along a nearby stream whose banks were covered with animal tracks. Here a coon had stopped to drink, there a skunk. Toads had left their faint scratchings as they hopped by, lizards their tail marks, and even worms their trails.

Much of the afternoon was spent exploring Forgotten Canyon. To reach its entrance involved a long waist-deep wade followed by a messy tramp over an oozing mud flat where, if you paused, you sank up to your knees. Trying to run over this was slightly nightmarish, but excruciatingly funny to the onlookers sitting safely on the bank.

That night we spread our sleeping bags close to the cliff on a ledge above the river, well out of the sand should it again blow. How strange and wonderful it was to see, no matter where one looked, not one sign of man, not even a road or trail to have brought us. These days most of us are so used to billboards along highways, to telephone poles against the skyline, to electric lights gleaming somewhere in the night, that we have come to accept them as a natural part of our surroundings. How astonishing at first is their absence. Nowhere that I looked at that minute could I see any light but that of the stars and our campfire close at hand, until I caught the glint of a flashlight whose owner was examining her sleeping site for foreign matter such as scorpions, black widows, and centipedes. Which again goes to show that what is one man's poison is another man's specimen.

I awoke to our fourth morning as a committee of five ducks in tight formation hurried down river, flying low over dawn's silver water. As I watched day drift down into our canyon world of melting shadows and slowly reddening cliffs, a large blue heron cruised by overhead, a few swallows darted about in the brightening sky, and the only sounds were the faint bustlings of that morning's cooking crew below on the sand bar. Now the evening film was being played backwards, the cloud colors going from pink to gold to white.

By then we were all well into the swing of the river-running routine, learning to keep our groans soft and indistinct as we crawled out into the icy morning air, to roll up our sleeping bags almost as we rolled out and to gather our scattered belongings and stuff them into our bags with the minimum of gestures, one eye still dozing. The cleverest of us even managed to cook breakfast in an unsuspected half-somnolent state. As beautiful as those dawns were, I am still content to leave them to that eager early bird and his worm.

The morning was calm and windless, so the boats were tied together side by side. Bargelike, we drifted with the current. We were suspended in a timeless world of our own, a box whose bottom was the brown river, whose sides were the sun-drenched reddish cliffs, and for a lid we had the sky. A thin line of willows and shrubby tamarisks grew along possible edges, offering a periodic touch of green, though usually the cliffs rose straight out of the water. An occasional beaver plopped into the water, disturbed by our passing, or a great blue heron flapped slowly on ahead. Otherwise we were alone.

This smiling sunny canyon world on such a lazy day wraps one in gossamer. Even now it slips by before my eyes and I see myself sprawled on the bow of the boat, watching it through half-closed lids. Fastened to the back of the big soft-voiced river, you can be still enough to belong. Everything is near and intimate. A hand can reach out to touch the river, touch a wall, almost touch the slice of sky. So completely are you part of the scene that you are no more aware of your minuteness than is an ant crawling along at the foot of a precipice. Not until you are home looking at photographs do you see how infinitely tiny you were at the base of the lofty wall.

This is a place of texture: the slippery shining surface of the river, the sandstone walls, the feathery fringes of the willows and tamarisks, the smooth pebbles scattered on sand bars, the dried, cracked mud. It is a place of color: burnished copper and gold, sand beige and pink, metallic black patches of shadow, soft greens. It is a place of form: flowing curves in slit side canyons, sweeps of domes and cave lips, pools of water in pockets, scraggly limbs of a dead sycamore. It is a place of reflections: bits of smooth water everywhere imprisoning pieces of sky, of cliff, of green leaves.

Out of the corner of an eye I glimpse a hawk. He flies by overhead and then sweeps up on a current of air, higher and higher, until suddenly he disappears over the top of the wall and is gone. How readily he does it—breaks the golden cord and goes out into that other unimaginable world outside, of whose existence he reminds me by his leaving.

Later that morning the boats were a hive of activity. Bill was busy pickling yesterday's haul of lizards and toads; our botanist was squashing flowers between sheets of newspaper; our ornithologist, with binoculars glued to her eyes, was scanning the passing cliff where someone thought he had sighted a jay; our anthropologist and geologist were poring over maps and muttering to each other in four-syllable words, our doctor was wandering precariously from boat to boat, camera in one hand and Band-Aids in the other; and members of the distaff side dreamed.

Midmorning we passed a huge jumble of rusted machinery, tons of it, stuck on a sand bar in the middle of the river. It is known as Stanton's Dredge. Many years ago it had been brought piecemeal, at a cost of more than one hundred thousand dollars, by wagon down a side canyon and then assembled, but the mining operation collapsed shortly afterwards, leaving this monument to failure that even the great floods of the Colorado have not been able to sweep away.

Later we pulled up to the bar at Hall's Crossing, clambered up the bank through the line of willows and brush, and crossed a flat open area to the foot of a high cliff. Here and there we

found agate and jasper flakes that the Indians had chipped off
the tools and arrowheads they were making, and fittingly, Bill
found a beautiful red jasper knife. Since we did not find any pottery, our anthropologist said that this was probably a hunting
site, called a non-ceramic site.

That afternoon in another side canyon, we saw a fairly well
preserved Indian ruin of several rooms built under an overhang
and at the top of a talus slope. The walls were made of flat slabs
of sandstone mortared together with mud in which fingerprints
were still visible. Small rocks, pieces of pottery and a few corn
cobs in a design were used as chinking. Covering one of the
rooms was a roof of cottonwood beams with layers of willow
poles and reeds. These had originally been covered with mud.
We also saw several bedrock metates, or wide grooves worn in
the sandstone by the Indians as they ground their corn.

Early the next morning, our fifth, we landed on an island.

An Anasazi ruin in Lake Canyon, tributary of the Colorado

From there we had to wade across a shallow branch of the river in order to get to the main shore. It was a biblical procession, with the bearded men, one after the other, striding purposefully along in waist-deep water, staffs in one hand and the book (their field notebooks) in the other, looking as if they were headed for nothing less than the Promised Land.

Here the canyon walls were sloping, one rounded ridge rising above another. Halfway up, under an overhang, was a ruin that our anthropologist tentatively identified as made by the Fremont Indians, another of the early Pueblo peoples that occupied this area along with the Anasazi, to whom most of the ruins we had so far seen had belonged. There were several rounded walls and two small neat igloo-type storage houses or granaries, perfectly preserved. Lying beside one was a sandstone slab shaped to fit over the opening. Under another overhang a seep turned the wall green with moss, cliff-rose, and Venushair fern. Such emerald niches were not uncommon and stood out in contrast to the bare red rock.

Climbing higher, we came upon a number of large bathtubs eroded out of the sandstone and filled with water. Strange tiny transparent creatures swam about, chased by water beetles. Bill identified them as fairy shrimp, an appropriate name for something so exotic. They practice the typical desert habitat cycle, their eggs lying potent but inert in the dust, maybe for years, until water brings them to life to start them on their way again. Around these pools Bill caught several treefrogs, or Hylas—though there wasn't a tree in sight—a pale-colored species that blended well with the sandstone. The sucker discs on their toes enabled them to cling as successfully to the perpendicular surface of rocks as to the bark and leaves of trees.

We then climbed to the rim of the canyon, up a long series of steps cut into the rock by a prospector who used to live nearby. In many places along the river faint remains of toe and hand holds called Moki steps can be seen leading up sheer walls, which were made and used by the Indians. On reaching the top and looking down, we could clearly see the demarcation of what millions of years ago had been various layers of shifting sand, criss-crossing each other as the wind blew. Cross-bedding, said our geologist.

Poor Bill was being paged by those at the top to "come quick, here's a lizard!" and by those still at the bottom to come quick as they had a bigger and better lizard. While watching Bill scrambling up and down, I heard our anthropologist say, "Thank heavens my pot shards don't have legs!"

Bill's activities were rewarded by the capture of two chuckwallas, large gray-black lizards that scuttle over the rocks, and when frightened, retreat to a crevice. There they puff themselves up so that it is almost impossible to dislodge them. The herpetologists, who wish them for specimens rather than for food, do not favor the Indian technique of puncturing them with a sharp stick in order to extract them from their hiding place, and therefore they must carefully pry away at the rocks. These lizards' fearsome looks belie their gentle natures. They are one of the few chiefly herbivorous desert species, most others eating arthropods or small vertebrates such as smaller lizards. Bill was delighted with these specimens, as he believed this area to be close to the northern limit of their range.

We also caught a bat hiding and squeaking in a hole. So we walked happily back to the boats, with a bat in a cigarette box, toads and lizards in knotted sacks, three fairy shrimp in a sun helmet, bunches of weeds tied up with string, pockets full of bits of jasper and agate, and what we hoped would be lovely pictures in our cameras.

Later that afternoon we came to the area known as the Rincon, a vast confusion of rock layers. Formations that we had left behind days ago suddenly reappeared, and our familiar Navajo sandstone that had been boxing us in for so many days had disappeared completely. We paused briefly near a cabin to exchange a few words with the custodian of some mining property and to pick up his mail. His radio was his only tie to the outside world, which in contrast to his own surroundings must have seemed to be a tangled and spidery place.

We saw our first and only snowy egret and later a large white pelican. This so surprised some of us that we yelled for the ornithologist, thinking we had discovered a record—a pelican so far from the sea. But apparently this species is not uncommon here, as it breeds on inland lakes.

On the sixth day we came to Hole-in-the-Rock, having paused earlier to look at some pictographs of strange figures in headdresses. Hole-in-the-Rock is one of the most famous crossings on the Colorado, and set into a slab of sandstone above the bank is a bronze plaque inscribed with the following words:

Mormon pioneers of the San Juan valley crossed the Colorado River at Hole-in-the-Rock January 26th 1880. Twenty-six wagons were lowered over the cliff that day. A total of 250 persons were in the party. All made the perilous descent and ferried the river here.

Four short sentences to commemorate one of the most dangerous and determined of pioneer treks. This group of Mormons, in search of new farmlands rumored available along the San Juan River, had arrived here after months of arduous travel over the rough canyon-dissected desert. What must have been their horror and despair on arriving at the edge of this last great canyon with a river far below! Undaunted, they managed the Herculean task of getting their wagons down to the floor of a side canyon. Next they built a road down it to the river's edge, and once there, a ferry to carry the wagons across, and then a road out on the other side. Even to our twentieth century eyes, or perhaps because of them, that historic undertaking seemed close to the miraculous.

At noon of that day we came to the junction of the Colorado and the San Juan, and it reminded us of an old proverb:

Tweed said to Twill, "What gars ye rin sae still?"
Twill said to Tweed, "Though ye rin wi' speed and I run slaw,
Yet where ye drown one man, I drown twa."

A meeting of rivers is always exciting. In a desert the fact that there is another river to meet is almost unbelievable.

We stopped for lunch at Hidden Passage, and after eating in a verdant dell under an overhang, we explored it. Seven years before, we had camped here, spreading our sleeping bags in a small dry wash out of the wind. During the night it rained and a flood of cold muddy water came down the wash to deluge us, a situation so classic on the desert that we should have known better.

Across the river is Music Temple, an enormous amphitheater carved out of the sandstone that magnifies and nourishes sound. Chiseled in the cliff one can read the name POWELL. In August of 1869 this indomitable one-armed geologist-explorer with a party of eight others made the first trip down the Colorado through the Grand Canyon, a feat of endurance and courage that ranks with the greatest. In all they floated down a thousand perilous miles of river through unknown country, beginning at the frontier town of Green River, Wyoming, and negotiating endless terrifying cataracts and rapids that have since drowned many men. In his journal Powell wrote:

> The features of this canyon are greatly diversified. . . . Sometimes, the rocks are overhanging; in other curves, curious, narrow glens are found. . . . Other wonderful features are the many side canyons or gorges that we pass. . . . Usually, in going up such a gorge, we find beautiful vegetation. . . . So we have a curious ensemble of wonderful features—carved walls, royal arches, glens, alcove gulches, mounds, and monuments. From which of these features shall we select a name? We decide to call it Glen Canyon.

A short time later we sighted Navajo Mountain looming blue-green above the canyon rim. This mountain, over ten thousand feet high, lies on the northwest edge of the reservation and figures as prominently in Navajo legend as it does in their scenery, for it is the home of their war god. The Indians block the wild animal trails leading up the mountain slopes so that their sheep will not wander to such a dangerous place.

After looking at some petroglyphs of sheep and a six-fingered hand, we walked up Twilight Canyon to another huge natural amphitheater. Nothing green grew here to soften or hide its structure as it had in Music Temple. It was pure architecture. Draw a horseshoe on a piece of paper. Imagine it to be five hundred feet across its two ends, thirteen hundred feet around the curve, with a cliff arching more than one thousand feet overhead; then imagine it filled with one hundred thousand people and you will have some idea of its size. To get a true picture though, you must paint your cliff a soft buff, stain it with long dark streaks hanging down like icicles from the rim, and across the opening put another cliff in luminous pink of reflected light, leaving only a small curved piece of sky on top. The thought that such a thing of beauty will be submerged when the dam is completed, depressed us anew.

Early morning of our seventh day we set off on foot up Forbidden Canyon, so named by the Navajos because of a landslide, a sign they interpreted to mean that their gods did not want them to trespass further. We had ample confirmation of their conviction seven years before when we camped under a sheltering overhang on a ledge above Forbidden Creek, and the canyon gods had expressed their disapproval of our trespassing by unleashing a cloudburst that almost swept us away. We awoke to the deafening roar of thunder, to constant lightning flashes that revealed a world awash and turned to silver. All around us glistening waterfalls fell from the canyon rims and crashed into the bottom below. The creek rose eight feet that night and carried away two of our boats and all of our food.

An offshoot of this canyon led to Rainbow Bridge, the world's largest natural bridge and the goal of our morning's hike. Bill offered to carry my sandwich in his snake bag providing I reached in to get it, but I decided to carry my own sandwich.

That day we felt more antlike than ever, crawling over the narrow canyon floor, back and forth across the creek from shadow to sun and back to shadow, with those high red walls on every side that varied so startlingly from deep red to delicate pink in the changing light. Gray-green buffalo-berry glistened in the sun, and the dainty purple aster waved as we passed. Snake-weed, daisies, and yellow peaweed lined our path, and we walked in and out of the honey scent of buckwheat. An occasional small redbud tree or two with heart-shaped leaves brushed against the sandstone walls, and the tall, even less frequent cottonwood caught at the sunlight and held it in glistening pieces.

Bill nabbed a striped whipsnake, which he kept removing from its sack to admire. He also trapped a number of fish: suckers and dace. Our botanist stuffed things into his collecting bag, and our ornithologist disappeared periodically in pursuit of a bird. Halfway up a few of us paused to swim in a long, narrow, cool-blue pool, disturbing the reflections as we moved. Somewhere hidden a canyon wren dropped its notes, as soft and liquid as the water in which we floated, dropped them into the sun-drenched silence. And so we floated in sound as well as in the water, lost in the bottom of the canyon world.

All around us was Indian land, the Indian land of our child-hood dreams where past and future have no meaning and loneliness is nonexistent, for here one cannot be other than part of everything. Time is but a series of "todays," as limitless and tiny as the grains of sand beneath our feet, that progress as methodically as the stars above and as irrevocably as the rocks are worn away below. Individual human identity as we visualize and practice it must be impossible for those who wander and wonder here. Belonging to the earth, their mother, they cherish the life-giving land as we have not yet learned to do. How inconceivable it would be to them to denude a forest, pollute a stream, destroy a river or lake.

As I was drying myself after our swim, I noticed a small gray bird with a short tail, sitting on a rock in the middle of the stream. Suddenly he plunged into the water and walked non-chalantly along the bottom picking up bits of food. When I later

Rainbow Bridge

recounted this astonishing performance to our ornithologist, I was informed that I had seen a water ouzel.

Then, just before noon, we rounded a corner and Rainbow Bridge spanned the sky. We walked until we stood in its shadow. High over our heads swept that great pink-red arc, shining against the sky. On the one hand, its very hugeness and complete simplicity of line were burstingly exhilarating; on the other hand, it pressed us down into the earth.

Though so gigantic when one is under it, from afar it is almost lost in the vast dimensions of the canyon walls. Specifically it measures 309 feet high, is 42 feet thick and 33 feet wide at the top, and stretches 278 feet from foot to foot, but I am not one who can translate figures into a picture. To our eyes it was no less astounding than to the eyes of the first white men who saw it in 1909.

That the water from the dam-created lake will come to its

very feet has provoked endless amount of discussion. There are those who believe that sudden immersion of the surrounding rock, dry for so many centuries, will have a disastrous effect; and there are the others who have convinced themselves that everything will be just fine. Fantastic protective measures have been suggested, involving the building of dams above and below the bridge along with a diversion tunnel to carry the creek waters around it down to the Colorado. It does not take much more than a glance at this country to realize the enormous proportions of such a project, not to mention the devastation the required machinery would wreak on the very scenery it was trying to save.

Around that night's campfire, as the firelight flickered on the cliff behind us, casting shadows that swayed and shivered, our boatman recounted an old Indian legend.

"Once upon a time, long ago when the world was young, there lived in this land a great chief. Besides many sheep and goats, he had a very beautiful wife whom he loved dearly. One day thick clouds rose up to cover the sun, and his wife sickened and died. The chief mourned her so greatly that in his grief he forgot his people. The Great Spirit summoned him to the Happy Hunting Ground to see his wife, and there she told him that he was being a bad chief to so cloud his eyes with tears for her that he could no longer see his people. The chief saw that he had done wrong and returned to his people determined to be a good and just leader. The Great Spirit wiped out his trail with the Colorado River so that he could not again go to the Happy Hunting Ground as a mortal. And so the Colorado was born." A few years later we were to see it die.

Past Driftwood Canyon, Quaking Bog, Cathedral, Little Arch, and Hanging Rope we went that eighth morning, seeing along the way two cormorants on a ledge. Later, in a canyon that had no name and which we subsequently called Catfish Canyon because of finding dozens of these trapped in a dwindling pool, we played with the echoes while the more energetic climbed up the side to investigate some Indian sites. The following morning we passed the Crossing of the Fathers marked by another bronze plaque. Here the two famous Franciscans made their arduous crossing in 1776. One can still see the steps hewn into the rock a short way up the narrow side canyon. A few miles farther were the remains of the survey stakes driven into the cliff by Robert Brewster Stanton, a prominent railroad engineer, during his disastrous expedition trying to survey these canyon walls as a possible site for a railroad. The tracks were to stretch from Colorado to California, somehow clinging to the canyon walls, even to those of the mighty Grand Canyon. This feat Mr. Stanton apparently never admitted as being either impractical or impossible.

Then we stopped at perhaps the most incredible of the many side canyons that we saw, called Labyrinth, and climbed over a large pile of rock rubble to reach the entrance. After a short distance the canyon's walls drew together making a narrow portal about two feet wide, at the bottom of which was a deep dark pool. One by one, with gasps and groans, we waded into it. The black icy water slowly crept up to our necks as we squeezed and inched our way along, cameras held high. Then up and out of the water we struggled, worked our way along a few more dark feet and back into another pool, this one not quite so deep. The walls of the passageway were draped with Venushair fern, red monkey-flower, cliff-rose, and the greenest of mosses, but in our wretchedness we were unappreciative of these charms. It ended in what is called Fatman's Misery, a constricted, twisted exit. That was only the beginning.

After a brief widening, which allowed us to catch our breaths, the canyon again narrowed to the most spectacular stretch of sinuous chasm that we had ever seen, an endless winding subterranean passageway, a twisting Gothic catacomb, an interlacing of fluted buttresses made by the rushing torrent swirling rocks around and around. Most of the time no sky was visible, for the canyon

Hidden Passage Canyon, now under the waters of Glen Canyon Dam

walls, stretching up hundreds of feet, never widened or straight-
ened, and were seldom more than a few feet apart. The half-light
filtering down revealed the many-faceted and -angled surfaces of
the walls that tilted and turned in every direction. Progress was
a matter of fitting one's body in and around, and we must have
looked, were it possible to see us, like a moving Egyptian frieze,
feet and head pointing forward and shoulders and hips facing
sideways, so narrow was the cleft. Enclosed in that dim cold world
of rock, all I could think of was: what if it rained and the canyon
filled up with water.

Later on the ninth afternoon we arrived at the dam site,
and under the startled eyes of a crew of steel-helmeted workers
trying to raise a truck out of the mud, we landed. Our anthropologist went off with the foreman in search of the boss with
whom our passage had been arranged, a matter of timing our
passing between blasts of dynamite!

Night descended and still we sat there in our boats, waiting
for that propitious moment. We watched the lights of the trucks
scurrying up and down the road that clung to the canyon wall,
with the giant cliff looming above them and the quiet light of the
stars beyond. High overhead we watched a tiny basket, fastened
to a cable strung from rim to rim, sail back and forth against the
night sky, hanging down from this spider's thread like some fragile
dewdrop. The small scattered patches of light were lost in the
enormous blackness; the busy man-made noises were lost in the
silence, like chicken-scratchings in a redwood forest. Man, with
his restless fingers, was picking away at eternity.

Inevitably, around that night's campfire, we contemplated
the Canyon's fate and passed again over the arguments which
streamed out from the basic man-pivoted premise: a great river
is a natural menace and must be converted to a natural resource.
That the Glen Canyon Dam is unnecessary is a well-documented
case, for its waters cannot be used for irrigation, and already the
three existing dams on the Colorado sufficiently control it and
provide ample hydroelectric power.

With the sound of man's fingerings still lingering in our ears, we had to ask ourselves as did Romain Gary: "Are we no longer capable of respecting nature or defending a living beauty that has no earning power, no utility, no object except to let itself be seen from time to time?" Perhaps in the dim recesses of his mind man is partly seeking revenge for his centuries of fear and helplessness; and like a child he shouts, "*Now* look at me!" as he knocks down another mountain. Aloud Bill wondered if this urge to use and destroy the world around him might not be a genetic characteristic, and if so, would he ever be able to control it? Then, after a pause, he added with a smile, "But archeology is an encouraging sign, where man is interested in something that cannot directly benefit him. Why, he actually shows an appreciation of past cultures for their own sake." And our anthropologist bowed to the assembled company as he went off to his sleeping bag.

Sometime later I was discussing the Glen Canyon Dam and particularly Rainbow Bridge with a newspaperman who waxed enthusiastic at the prospect of this somewhat inaccessible country being, as he called it, "opened up." In his opinion it would be just grand to have a paved highway leading to the foot of the Bridge itself so that all one had to do was to roll down the automobile window. What cannot be seen by everyone with little or no effort, for him had no value, and a wilderness uncut by roads was therefore a needless waste. But, as Aldo Leopold pointed out, "Recreational development is a job not of building roads into lovely country but of building receptivity into the still unlovely human mind."

The wilderness today is available to almost everyone, and those who care enough will see it. "And caring," says my husband, "they may be more inclined to leave it undamaged and unlittered. But even more important than man's actually seeing it, I think, is the fact that it is there and a man knows that it is there, for him to dream about." Imprisoned inside his cities, he needs a herd of elephants wandering freely through a forest, a seething

Entrance to Labyrinth, a side canyon now underneath Lake Powell

Colorado churning in the bottom of a canyon, a flock of migrating geese calling out of the cold night sky, "We're here, all's right with the world." For "The wilderness and the idea of wilderness is one of the permanent homes of the human spirit" (Joseph Wood Krutch).

That night the northern lights rose above the canyon walls, a pink glow slashed with ever-widening and -narrowing streaks of white. In the silence of the night, at the bottom of the encompassing canyon, they were eerily and terrifyingly awesome. It seemed to us that the rest of the world was on fire and in the end nature would reclaim its own. And man, will he be a long time passing?

Our last day could not have been more winning. No sky was ever bluer, no clouds ever whiter as they chased each other across the blue chasm above, no river carried one more peacefully or more inevitably onward. Some of us took to air mattresses, and half in the water we glided along between massive sandstone walls laid down when dinosaurs strode among the trees and flying reptiles mottled the sky.

I remembered a diagram I used to puzzle over as a child, depicting neatly the Tree of Life, beginning with minute things adrift in an ocean, moving up the branches to me. But not until this trip had I really felt the earth's great age, the long procession of life upon its surface. In the 150 miles we had just traveled, over 150 million years had slipped by in the windings of this river. We had brushed our hands over rock that marked the golden age of the amphibians, over rock that marked the dying of the dinosaurs and the materialization of a few mousy little creatures in whose brains flickered unbelievable things to come. I could not help but wonder whose hand, if a hand at all, would a long time hence brush over the rock made from sand on which we ourselves had walked.

Caught in the current, in the pull towards the sea, we were returning to our birthplace. Step by step down the ladder, that long tortuous history would pass again before our eyes in the layers of the girdling rock; we felt it coursing through our veins. And I saw myself, formless, floating in the warm sea womb.

As I sit writing, the dam is finished, the water is slowly rising in Glen Canyon, submerging the rare and beautiful things we once saw, and the Colorado River, now only a trickle of its former self, flows gently southward. The last time I listened to the ranger on the rim of the Grand Canyon, he told his impressed audience of the mightiness of the Colorado, how you could hear it roar from miles away and see the spray it tossed up as it passed, how it had inexorably cut its way down through thousands of feet of rock. "But best of all," he concluded triumphantly, "this canyon is still in the making!"

Now all that is changed, the river's back broken by man-made levers, its silty violence no longer there to chisel away at primeval rock, no longer there for man to think upon. Had he been able to get to it sooner, he might have prevented the river's forming any great canyon at all, and somewhere else, perhaps, he's preventing a future one.

As I sit writing, plans are being made for other dams, one to flood the great and magnificent Marble Canyon that lies between the Glen and the Grand, and even one that will flood a section of the Grand Canyon itself! How this can be in the face of all that man has lost, all that he now knows, and what he at last is beginning to realize about the earth, is wholly incomprehensible.

Like a magic refrain the names of the many side canyons we saw during that trip go drifting through my mind: Forgotten, Twilight, Mystery, Music Temple, Hidden Passage, Labyrinth, Forbidden, Cathedral. If we should say them to our children, will they forgive us for having drowned them all in water? Were I they, "I should not like to think that some demigod had come before me and picked out some of the best stars" (Thoreau).

Summer clouds beginning to build up for a storm

8

Summer

SUMMER is what the true lover of the desert impatiently awaits. When the thermometer tops the 100-degree mark, usually in May, those who find the heat intolerable head for higher ground, the Pacific Coast, or withdraw sulkily into their air-conditioned houses not to reappear until fall. Summer—and it lasts a good five months—has a peculiar ambiance of its own, and its devotees have all the earmarks of any cultist. Listen to them talking in their patios of an evening, bragging about how they dig postholes when it's 110 degrees, how they drive across the Yuma desert in July with all the windows open, how, when they're alone in the house, they would never think of turning on the cooler. The outsider, he who retreats in the face of the first searing blast, they view with pity and scorn. "He just can't take it," they say, shaking their heads for the weak thing that he is.

Of course, this is the appeal. It is the old story of man pitting himself against nature. The game comes to an end in the face of technology as definitely as it does if the player calls quits and leaves, for few can derive the same satisfaction from a battle fought for him by machines as he can and does from one won by his own ingenuity and courage.

I remember once driving across the bleached and baking desert northwest of Tucson. The dusty ground was cracked with only a scattering of small-leafed shrubs shriveled to their very bones. The heat blurred the horizon and shimmered on the road ahead of us, leaving mirage-pools of water on the pavement. An occasional puff of hot wind stirred up the dust into small twisters that zigzagged in and out of a few bushes before collapsing. The temperature in the shade was close to 115 degrees and the inside of the car was indistinguishable from an oven. My dark glasses so burned my nose that I could hardly wear them, and the enveloping heat was such that I was in an insensible daze. I could have been stuck with a pin and I wouldn't have felt it. My only thought was to rewet periodically the strip of rag wrapped around my neck. This, due to the process of evaporation, is supposed to make one feel cooler! Then it was that my husband, beaming with good cheer, said to me after taking a deep breath of the fiery air, "Isn't this great! Now *this* is really living!"

The desert summer does not kindle in my breast the same enthusiasm that it does in the breast of my husband. Sitting far removed from it beside a winter fire with a cold wind whistling outside, I think I can appreciate the strange exhilaration that comes from successfully meeting the challenge of the summer elements, much as one might react to a hurricane or a blizzard, but when actually faced by it I persevere dumbly and ingloriously; and I wish I were somewhere else.

In the old days before refrigeration, it mattered how your house was built. Ideally, the most practical construction for keeping out the desert heat came to us from the Arabs by way of the southern Spaniards and the conquistadors. This was a thick-walled, high-ceilinged house, windowless on the outside, and built around an unroofed square. All rooms opened out onto this central patio which was filled with plants and in the center of which usually splashed a fountain, a cool effect on ear and eye.

Failing this the house should at least present little of its surface to the western sun and that as unbroken by glass as possible, and the eaves should overhang wherever necessary to shade windows and walls alike. But whatever the style of architecture, much can be done with trees and vines judiciously planted and awnings and blinds judiciously arranged to keep the sun from touching the house sides. It is surprising how much one can fool the eye into thinking that it is cooler than it actually is, not only with outside green and shade, but with blue and green slipcovers inside. And by removing rugs, bare feet can walk on cool cement or brick floors.

So the game is played if you have only a swamp cooler, a metal box whose sides and back are of padded excelsior through which water seeps and a fan blows, forcing out air cooled by evaporation. This contraption works well enough when the humidity is below fifteen per cent. It brings to mind one of the most exasperating of all dogmas perpetrated by the lovers of the summertime. "It is never uncomfortably hot here," they blandly claim. "The heat's so dry you don't even feel it." This is a dire euphemism, for the summertime is also our rainy season, and when the thermometer is over a hundred it does not take much humidity to incapacitate the swamp cooler along with human beings.

Yet I am almost romantic enough to say that I too prefer the days before the refrigerated house and car. The ritual and rhythm of a summer day that began with the shutting of the windows, the lowering of the blinds, and the watering of the garden, was pleasantly soothing. Then life was geared to the elements in a way that it no longer is in its artificial coolness. Man adapted himself to his surroundings by perseverance and mutual respect, not by the superimposition of a manufactured environment. Then life had a leisure that now can be found only south of the border. One did one's business in the early morning and late afternoon, and midday one withdrew behind closed shutters and slept. Not until after sunset did the daytime troglodytes reappear to gather with their friends in the patios and sit under the stars, admiring the night as well as their own fortitude.

The desert animals follow very much this same routine. They hide in holes during the heat of the day and carry on their business in the early morning and late afternoon hours if they are diurnal, and at night if they are otherwise inclined, though some animals may be both nocturnal and diurnal depending on the time of year. I am crepuscular.

Often in the late afternoon we will go down and sit by the stream. Let us say that it is June, summer well under way. The boys are accompanying me in order to catch a variety of invertebrates to restock the aquarium. For this purpose each is armed with a tea strainer and pail. As we walk out the door I again notice the neat holes in the leaves of the lilac bush where the leaf-cutting bees have been at work. They fly off with an oval piece of my lilac leaf curled up between their legs and with it line a cell of their nest. Into this insulated green cavity they stuff pollen and finally lay an egg floating in a few drops of nectar.

The plums are ripening on the plum tree. Every night a rock squirrel helps himself, leaving his pits meticulously lined up on the wall so that I can count exactly how many he took. We hear the mournful cry of an ever hopeful bachelor quail, and as we pass the saguaro, we step across a thronged ant highway. Parked on either side of it are two horned toads eagerly licking up the ants as they hurry to and fro; and they are still at it some hours later, looking fat and pleased. Each arm of the saguaro is tipped with an untidy cluster of fruit. These split open revealing a red inside and are often mistaken for flowers. Once I asked Peter, then six, what the saguaros looked like to him in this condition and he promptly replied, "Like the man who hasn't combed his hair with Wildrood Cream Oil."

Papago Indians, whose reservation is to the west of Tucson, eat the fruit raw or make it into a preserve. They also ferment the juice into a kind of wine. Inside the fruit are tiny black seeds which, being rich in fat, the Indians make into a butter-like spread. These seeds are also one of the favorite foods of the white-winged dove.

The hot desert winds have dried up all the juicy spring

green, and only a fringe is left along the edges of the stream which has shrunk to a trickle choked with snakelike streamers of algae that undulate in the faint current. One large pool is still left, spreading out from under a sycamore tree, but the very much smaller pools downstream from it are more suitable to the boys' purpose, so we first stop there. In the typical fashion of desert streams this one has reached the point where it is now mostly underground. It appears bubbling icy cold out between the rocks above the large pool and it disappears back into the sand several hundred yards downstream.

The first thing that catches my eye are a few black, shiny, whirligig beetles skating madly about on the surface in ever-changing patterns as with their specially modified eyes they peer both above and below the water for things to eat. I stop at this particular pool to see what else might be sharing it with them, and the boys each choose a different one a couple of yards away. Theirs, as well as mine, to judge from their comments, is a terrifying jungle of life. The tiny creatures that prowl through the dwindling watery forests of algae are fiercer and more voracious than any tiger.

First I watch the diving beetles, which are similar in appearance to the whirligigs skimming above them. Being air breathers, they carry a small silver air bubble attached to their posteriors, which they use like an aqua-lung. They are continuously swimming back and forth between the bottom, where they forage, and the top, where they collect a fresh bubble by thrusting their tail-ends above the surface. Two other equally active and therefore noticeable creatures are the popeyed backswimmers and the water boatmen. The former hangs head down from the surface, with his rear end in the air and his long lanky hind legs stuck out like oars. These he uses to scull himself along upside down in the jerky rhythm of a breast stroke. I watch one dive down, a silver lining of air clinging to the underside of his body. I see another holding on to a swaying grass-stem with his front legs, which because of his inverted position look as if they sprout out from the top of his head. The water boatmen, darting about, give somewhat the same effect as backswimmers, and in this pool they are more numerous.

While I am watching a snail creep over a stone, a nearby twig begins to move. It is a water scorpion stalking stealthily along in search of a succulent victim, for like many insects he eats by sucking. He has a snorkel tube at the end of his body, which he sticks above the water whenever he is at rest and needs air.

My pool has both mayfly and dragonfly nymphs lurking in the algae. These greedy creatures with the deceptively romantic names may live as long as a year in the water before assuming their final shape. The mayfly nymph looks a little like a pale yellowish helicopter as it moves slowly through the water, and the dragonfly nymph, a thoroughgoing carnivore, very slightly resembles the creature it will at last become. After about a half-dozen molts one

Michael and Hugh catching aquatic insects

can see traces of the future wings beneath the clear outer skin. I ask the boys if they want either of these for the aquarium, but they have plenty in their own pools.

Peter discovers a giant water bug. Its back is covered with eggs and he naturally concludes that it is a female. But nature has a sly way of fooling you, and this turns out to be a male. I think about the midwife toad and even more about the sea horse and I speculate on the titillating evolutionary trend that saddles the male with the maternal duties. Peter also collects some snail eggs, a mass of clear jelly adhered to a stone. A hand lens will change each black speck imbedded in the jelly into an infinitesimal snail. And under a rock he finds a lovely crayfish. Could we find enough of them I would be tempted to try my hand at *Gratin de Queues d'Ecrevisses Nantua*.

John, in his pool, first finds a larva of the caddis fly, also appropriately called the stick worm, for it builds itself a tube, in which it lives, by cementing together with saliva bits of leaves and gravel. Next he finds a long hairlike creature called a hairsnake, or horse-hair worm, because it was popularly believed to be a horse hair come to life. In a series of seemingly impossible coincidences the life cycle of this animal unfolds, beginning with the laying of the eggs on plant material that is then eaten by an insect such as a grasshopper or a cricket. The eggs hatch and the worm lives in the body cavity of its host, awaiting the day that it comes in contact with water so that it can emerge.

Mike concentrates on catching tadpoles, and Hugh on pouring water over himself with his pail. At last the boys decide they have enough specimens and they walk home. I warn them to be sure and separate their catches wisely so as to keep the mortality rate to a minimum. One might assume that an aquarium would be the one place from which animals would not wander, but I have found this not to be true. I have chased whirligig beetles and backswimmers as they fly around the living room, as well as dragonflies and mayflies who have unexpectedly reached the final stage. The first time this happened I was amazed, just as I was amazed to see water boatmen and backswimmers swimming around in our freshly filled pool, but of course, with wings, a great deal is possible. Just the other day I came upon a mayfly poised on the surface of our aquarium with its shed skin floating beside it, and as I watched, it flew away.

Alone I walk up to a large pool. It is alive with small non-native mosquito fish, but I also catch a glimpse of a native dace or two. In another couple of weeks the water will be gone and so perforce will they. Not all pools dry up, however. Some, chiefly higher up in the canyons, are present all year round and from such as these come our fish. Visitors to the Museum are always astonished to learn that the desert nurtures native fish, some highly adapted to our extremes of temperature. For example: the pup fish which occurs in desert pools can live in temperatures up to 100 degrees Fahrenheit.

I sit on the small beach with the water at my feet. Doves call, and quail, and upstream a young horned owl squeaks his hunger. It reminds me of the time when such a sound sent me running for the stepladder, the forceps, and the horsemeat. The Mexican ground doves come flying swiftly through the trees for their evening drink, lighting on the sand and then bobbing hurriedly up to the water's edge. The mourning doves come too, with excited twittering and soft wings brushing the air, and also the white-wings, pausing on the dead branches of a nearby tree for a look-around. Towhees hop from bushes down to the ground and back up to the bushes with unceasing energy. A kingbird, his pale yellow breast catching the sun, sits for a while on a hackberry's highest branch, cocking his head this way and that just as Margalo, perched on Peter's shoulder, used to do. Below him sits a thrasher and below him a cardinal. The tree is tiered with birds. A Bullock's oriole dashes past, flashing his gaudy colors. He has probably been eating the grapes by the kitchen door. Then comes a Cooper's tanager almost lost among the several cardinals, and as if this riot of color is not yet enough, a vermilion flycatcher flits by with his mate. I hear the faint whirring of a hummingbird and suddenly I see him poised on a twig not far away.

The bright, harsh, yellow light has softened, and the day ripens like a fruit growing full and golden. I hold it heavy and warm, in a languid hand. The splashes of gold on the yellow-green grass that covers the opposite bank under the willows move slowly up into the trees as the sun lowers behind me. Our world is a patchwork of green and gold, sun and shadow. These ripples of color throb and murmur and are fused with the drone of a passing orange-winged tarantula-hawk. This wasp, which has a very painful sting, is probably out looking for a tarantula to paralyze so that she can lay her egg on it; but I do not think of this, suspended as I am in this shallow virescent sea.

I can see a lizard scuttle up the rough trunk of a nearby ash, and ants, with blatant purposefulness, are every-which-waying over the sand on which I sit. Gnats buzz around my ears and I scratch and swish the air with a willow branch. I hear two quail lightly chattering to each other, and the male appears around a grass clump, followed by his mate. They hurry along on twittering legs, two dapper little *petits bourgeois,* and take their places at the water's edge among the doves and towhees, but they do not loiter as the others do. Another quail is drinking by the sycamore, a mother with five babies. When she finishes she scurries off, followed by her troop who scramble to get in line behind her. Two gilded flickers land on a branch, one just below the other, and tap a few times before they are off. And everywhere are those small gray bird-birds, all of which my husband calls dickey-birds.

Now only the tops of the trees are gold, and now all is in shadow except the very crest of a faraway hill. Three or four buzzards, high where the sun still clings, wheel slowly in lazy horizontal spirals. They wheel clockwise, and I wonder if below the equator they wheel counter-clockwise according to the Coriolis force. A few nighthawks nervously swoop down to catch a drink, as does a purple martin. The latter makes three or four passes, banking to one side and then the other as he goes, and then he plays awhile above the trees, tumbling about in the silky air. Then come the bats. I can see them only when they are silhouetted against the pale gray-blue sky. Against the trees, they are only barely suspected, fluttering shadows. The warm air is intermittently pushed away by a cool breath off the water that smells moist and mustily of algae.

Now the bird activity has ceased, all but the doves gossiping and flapping their wings as they settle down for the night. The insects take over where the birds have left off: the cicadas in an incessant rasp, and the tree crickets. One places one's ear against these vibrations much as one might place a finger on a pulse beat. A distant rooster crows, and the sounds of the outer world grow louder and penetrate more deeply: a far-off plane, someone hammering, a dog barking, and boy voices dropping like pebbles into the cool pool of evening.

Then I see a star, a small one twinkling uncertainly above the hackberry. If I look away I shall lose it in the yet too-light sky. And so we hang, day not quite done, night not quite come, until an owl glides silently by, close overhead, trailing behind him the whispering dark.

Perhaps this will be the night the cereus will bloom. I remember once, sitting at dinner, when the sliding glass doors were pushed back, and a warm wind brought to us as we were leisurely eating our dessert a sweet, sweet odor. Suddenly Bill came to. "Why, the cereus must be in bloom!" And he jumped up and went rushing off into the desert. Being more cautious, I had to get a flashlight before following him, as I had no intention of stepping on a rattlesnake if I could avoid it. We spent the next hour or so sniffing the air and then, like bird dogs, closing in on the blooming cacti. That night we literally smelled out almost a dozen cereus. They are as symbolic of the desert as anything that I can imagine. Every day of the year except one or two they are a shabby, scraggly plant hidden away under a mesquite tree, where it looks like a dead stick. Then one evening in June a number of insignificant buds unfold into large, many-petaled, waxy white flowers that are as exotic as water lilies, and this desert of ours smells like a garden in the Arabian Nights.

June is a month of waiting. It is our most uncomfortable month, hot, increasingly humid (for the desert) as the rainy season nears, and exasperating. Every day we hopefully watch the clouds mushroom up from behind the mountains and then subside. Every night we listen to the distant thunder and watch the lightning threaten the mountains, which at this time of year are tinder-dry. One does not need to have lived here long to have seen the telltale column of smoke by day and the column of fire by night, and none of us will easily forget the year the whole mountain range to the south seemed to be burning. We could see its ribs outlined by the fire, and I half expected the whole structure to crumble as might a building.

At last even the water hole under the sycamore dries up and all that is left is a cupful of water where a coyote has scratched in the damp sand. Bees and wasps gather there, and on our approach the persistent garter snake slides up into the overhanging roots.

During those anticipatory weeks I live in a state of suspended inertia and I take the infuriating unfruitfulness of the clouds as a personal and malevolent gesture of nature itself. I am full of impotent rage. But this tension is miraculously dispelled on the day of the first rain. San Juan's Day, June 24, is supposed to initiate this event, but it very rarely does. The first rain is more likely to come at the beginning of July, but on a bad year it won't come until later, and sometimes it hardly comes at all. This is a hardship for both the desert and its inhabitants, including the rancher who depends on the summer grass to feed his cattle.

June, however, is good for one thing: it is good for snake-hunting. It is then that the rarest and most elusive of the snakes will wander and can be captured as they cross the roads at night.

Until this technique was discovered some years after the advent of the automobile, very few specimens of the nocturnal species had been taken. Now we may find six or seven leaf-nosed snakes in one evening alone. So we drive slowly along, carefully examining the road ahead for the significant wriggle of a snake. I tend to daydream as we cruise through the night, and our car becomes a boat sailing over an endless ribbon of time. Then screech, jerk, bump, pick yourself off the dashboard while the driver hurtles out of the car and down the road, flashlight in hand, to throw himself on an eight-inch length of reptile. Back he comes, stuffing his prize into a snake sack and asking me for the temperature. I then remember my numbed hand that is sticking out the window with the thermometer. Providing the time of year is right, a definite correlation exists between the number of snakes about and the air temperature as well as the state of the moon. The best snake-hunting nights are those in June before the rainy season begins, when the temperature is in the mid-80's, and during the dark of the moon. The nocturnal species are less inclined to prowl on bright nights.

A typical summer day will go something like this. We wake to a brilliant blue and cloudless sky and listen to the weather forecast: continued warm, variable cloudiness with chance of afternoon and evening thunder showers, mostly over the mountains; last night's low 76, today's expected high 101. By midmorning every high mountain range is capped with a small flat-bottomed cloud. As the day advances, the one cloud becomes two, then three. They join, expand, rise up, and then melt back to a small dispirited heap. They re-form, and once again, with renewed vigor, they billow up, and a few slide forward on the table of hot air. Each day their struggle against the dissolving blasts of heat is repeated, and each day, like balloons, they bravely puff themselves up in the face of the burning sun. Towards early afternoon they are piled thick and high on the horizon in the bumptious turmoil of corralled animals. Then they surge forward, the ones behind sometimes overleaping the leaders in the bounding eagerness of their flight. Their flat undersides turn dark and lightning is violently squeezed out as they jostle and shove. They spread out, swell up larger and larger, and turn black. Watching, we are caught in the excitement of their tumult. A sharp-winged hawk flies swiftly by, a small silhouette against the brooding storm, and later two doves in search of shelter.

Finally a gray filmy curtain is lowered from the clouds closest to the mountains, and we watch it move slowly towards us. First comes the wind, blowing clouds of dust before it and bringing the odor of wet creosote. A forgotten door slams, and then we hear the preliminary large heavy drops upon the roof. Immediately we are in the middle of a downpour. We can see nothing but lashing rain. It slackens, it renews, it slackens. In twenty minutes a half-inch of rain has fallen and then all is quiet. The storm has gone roaring off to the southwest, and five or six miles down the road it will dwindle and disintegrate. South Tucson will not get a drop. Its hot cheeks will be fanned briefly by a cool moist wind and that is all.

The temperature outside the house has dropped to 80. We quickly open all the windows, but an hour later the sun is out and the thermometer again rises. By sunset the sky is nearly as clean and tranquil as it was in the early morning, deceptively so, for after nightfall we can hear thunder rumbling in the distance. We walk up to the crest of our western hill, and from our grandstand seats we can see incipient storms grumbling over every mountain range. Sometimes the play of lightning is stupendous. Almost without interruption flash after blinding flash stabs the far flanks of the mountains. Long and short, thin and thick, mostly perpendicular but sometimes flickering horizontally across the sky, the flashes cut up the horizon in an ancient mythological war, and we marvel.

Often, though, the great black clouds will rush on by us to drop their cooling contents elsewhere. The mountains then in the humid air gather about them a shawl of shifting vapors through whose fringes they appear softened, many-layered and unfamiliar. A beam of white light will pick out a patch of distant cliffs and boulders and magnify them so that they seem astoundingly close and intimate. Or perhaps a certain canyon, suddenly disclosing newly discernible depths, will capture the eye and lead it past misty stone buttresses back into dim recesses haunted by pale amorphous creatures. And our mountains are of another time and another place.

If the downpour has been particularly heavy, a real cloudburst, we venture forth by car to see the damage. The streets then are rivers, cars are stalled, people are standing in doorways with shovels and brooms. We plow through the brown water like a tugboat. In places the flat desert outside of the city is a shining gray lake and every crease is running, joining others, swelling, pouring into the washes that are muddy boiling rivers. It is impossible to believe that the desert can ever be so wet and its dry

Our stream after a flood

rivers ever be so full of water. And it is equally impossible to believe that the torrents can so quickly again be dry, for five or six hours later only a layer of wet mud will be left.

If our own stream is dry at the onset of the summer rainy season, we anxiously await its refilling. After the first heavy downpour in the mountains that feed it, we listen for the warning roar that heralds its coming and then rush down just in time to see the tongue of water coated with foam come around the bend. It is always an exciting moment. Minutes later the water will be two or three feet deep. Because our stream is wide, the so-called head of water is only a few inches high and moves with about the speed of a walking man. It takes a narrow canyon to produce the proverbial wall of water.

With the coming of the rains our tempo again changes. The afternoons are usually cooler even if the rain has fallen elsewhere. People begin to stir about once more. During a good rainy season everyone is marvelously cheerful. Almost every afternoon a storm inundates some piece of desert, and every conversation begins by comparing the amount of rain one house has had with that of another. One year downtown Tucson will get most of the rain and another year the east side. At best it is spotty, but we are grateful for every drop.

And as the people revive and begin to stir, so will the animals. Driving along the road at night one can see all kinds of things: high-stepping tarantulas that look as big as saucers, yellow scorpions, the orange and black giant desert centipede, the glint off the eyes of a wolf spider, pocket mice, kangaroo rats. The latter is a fascinating animal, with abnormally enlarged hind legs similar to the kangaroo (hence its name), that has adapted itself so well to desert living it can exist without drinking water. What it needs is supplied by the water of metabolism, resulting from the oxidation of various foods within its body. And sometimes we will see a skunk or a large-eyed, ring-tailed cat, not a cat at all but a member of the raccoon family. This dainty creature was so named by the early miners because it proved to be such an excellent mouser. But most of all we see toads.

One of the most interesting of all the desert life-cycles takes place during the summer rains, in fact is dependent on them. It is that of the spadefoot toad. The whole thing unfolded before our eyes during our second summer on the desert. We had just finished building a small cement birdbath outside our living-room window when the first rain of that summer occurred, obligingly filling the basin for us. Even before the rain had stopped I heard the unmistakable lamblike bleat of a spadefoot coming from the direction of our new birdbath, and on looking out the window I saw a toad swimming about with a splotch of white below his chin as he filled his air sac to call. A spadefoot, definitely a spadefoot. Soon another male had joined him and then several more. Like magic they appeared out of the ground.

Down at the freshly running stream the same thing was happening. Its edges were lined with spadefoots bleating away in a frenzy of excitement. Others swam this way and that, frantically trying to decide where to settle, and whenever one approached the bank he would be accosted by an already established toad who, thinking the newcomer a female lured by his call, would eagerly swim out and clasp him amorously without any introductions whatsoever. Then there would be a slight flurry in the water during which the aggressor was rudely shrugged off, and both toads would quickly head towards the bank to begin calling. As usual the females played hard-to-get, and it wasn't until several hours later that they began to appear. By morning every submerged blade of grass and stick along the edges of the stream was coated with caviarlike eggs imbedded in jelly, and so too was the birdbath. By the following morning the eggs had hatched and tiny tadpoles were swimming about. The whole cycle from the time of the laying of the eggs to that of the tadpole turning into a toad is amazingly quickened in order to take place during the two weeks or less that the temporary desert pools usually last. In a damper climate the cycle of related toads may exceed a month.

A Sonora green toad calling

Though the spadefoot best or most dramatically illustrates the adaptation to desert conditions, all of our toads breed during this time of year. I remember our fourth wedding anniversary, which started out appropriately enough with champagne and steak at a downtown restaurant. Half-way through dinner it began to thunder so loudly that even buried in the bowels of the building in which we were eating, we could hear it. My husband grew more and more restive until, just before the dessert, he excused himself and went to survey the exterior conditions. He returned with the news that a humdinger of a cloudburst was raging outside, "and this is the night the toads will really be out," he concluded. Thirty minutes later we were prowling around in the mud that edged the flooded eastside garbage dump after frogs, I mean toads, me in high heels and a pink embroidered dress sent to me by my mother for my twenty-sixth birthday. Never had I heard such a racket. It was a toad bedlam. The spadefoots were bleating, the larger Great Plains toads were contributing an incessant earsplitting trill and the Colorado River toads a weak, wheezing, steamboat whistle. The water was filled with amorous toads and they also seemed to be everywhere that I was about to step. We caught a lot of toads that night, or rather my husband did. I held the flashlight.

Last summer a huge Colorado River toad laid beautiful strings of black egg-beads on the swimming pool steps; we heard the love-sick male calling early in the morning from the pool. That afternoon one of the boys came in to report a dead horned toad in the play yard; a house-guest, overhearing the news, innocently asked if that was the poor toad who had been in the swimming pool. "No," said my husband, a compulsive punster, "that one was a horny toad."

Besides toads, the summer rains also bring out flowers and grass. I have a picture of my husband standing on the bank of our stream with sunflowers reaching head-high, a good six feet. The most common grass is the aforementioned six-weeks grama, and the most common flowers are the perennial white zinnias and the yellow paper-flowers that cover beautiful small symmetrical bushes. Also conspicuous is the Arizona poppy, or caltrop. This is not a poppy at all but a relative of the creosote and looks startlingly like the gold-poppy which grows in the early spring under the influence of the winter rains.

But perhaps the summer brings out most obviously the insects and spiders. (Spiders, which have eight legs, are not insects, which have only six, but both are arthropods.) Everywhere one walks one is likely to see a "bug" that one has never before seen. Only last summer I was astonished to look down and see beautiful red velvety creatures, about the size and shape of a ladybird beetle, crawling about on the ground. John put some in his pocket for his father to identify, and they turned out to be velvet mites, one of the largest of the mites.

It is impossible to read at night without the light being ringed with winged creatures. A cardinal rule is never to read in bed. That is another reason why I do not like the summers. We often play badminton at night, and the lights attract an enormous number of whatever is current at the time. For example, in July the June bug, more specifically called the May beetle, is most prevalent. These litter the court, much to the delight of the large Colorado River toad, who hops around licking them up. Another of these toads usually stations himself under the back-door light, which successfully attracts a sizable dinner for him

These toads most people find repugnant, but in their ample ugliness lies a perverse charm. What might make them legitimately less attractive are the skin glands that secrete a digitalis-like substance, poisonous if taken internally. This should pose no threat to humans, but it does pose a threat to dogs, who are often tempted to seize them playfully, with resulting convulsions from which they may not recover. My husband's position on this subject is that dogs can be trained to leave them alone and therefore dog owners should refrain from killing this beneficial toad who is such a dedicated pest controller.

The beetle that most effectively disturbs my nighttime badminton game is a large long-horned beetle. It comes plunging onto the court like a flying tank and then stalks about, gesticulating with its long antennae. The only thing about it that might possibly earn it a small amount of sympathy is the fact that it spends up to three years as a larva and only two weeks as an adult, an unfair proportion I think, unless one believes childhood to be the choicest stage. On considering its eating habits, however, my original antipathy is renewed. As larvae these beetles spend their time feeding on the roots of the lovely palo verde tree, sometimes killing it, and in this phase they are known as the palo verde wood borer. As adults they do not eat at all. Another beetle that comes avisiting is one of the carabids. This carnivorous ground beetle scurries around eating whatever it can find, dead or alive, and between it and the Colorado River toad the badminton court is licked clean.

I remember the evening I had actually managed to win fifteen points from my husband and was just about to serve, when he said, "It's not fair that I should have to play against two!" Next to me was a big black tarantula waving its front legs. I promptly lost the game.

In the summer the male tarantula is out looking for a female; and out looking for them both is the tarantula-hawk, a large, fierce black wasp with orange wings. On finding a tarantula this insect paralyzes it with its sting and then drags it down a hole where it glues an egg to the victim's skin. The spider remains alive for a number of weeks in a state of suspended animation, thus providing fresh meat for the wasp larva. It is this visible abundance of life, as well as the flagrant heat, that prevents you from ignoring the natural world outside your window as you can ignore it during the winter calm. The desert summer vibrates before your eyes and forces you to note its existence.

Every September, with baleful eye, Bill sniffs the hot breeze and somehow therein detects an imaginary taint of coming coolness. "Humph!" he says, "there's a winter chill in the air." My husband's only irascible articulations, except for those brought on by the borrowing and not returning of his possessions, are made about the winter weather. He usually concludes these with a remark such as: "Those poor devils who come out here for the winter just don't know any better, I guess. It's just like the inhabitants of hell summering in Death Valley to escape the heat, though I can't imagine why they should want to leave for that reason!" No wonder that one of his favorite poems is "The Cremation of Sam McGee," which takes place in the furnace of an old boat wrecked on the shore of a Yukon lake:

> And there sat Sam, looking cool and calm, in the
> heart of the furnace roar;
> And he wore a smile you could see a mile, and
> he said: "Please close that door.
> It's fine in here, but I greatly fear you'll let in
> the cold and storm—
> Since I left Plumtree, down in Tennessee, it's
> the first time I've been warm."

My husband and Sam are kindred spirits, and once again I can hear Bill say as he breathed deeply of the burning air blowing through our car that stifling July day, "Isn't this great! Now *this* is really living."

"Clover Leaf" in the Pinacate

9

Camping

IN Arizona we are particularly fortunate, for only a little farther than the proverbial stone's throw from our twentieth century bustle are many areas still wild, unlittered, and relatively unexplored, areas ideal for camping; and of all the many activities that the desert enhances, camping is my favorite. It is the soft sound of busy birds and insects, the sun changing the shadows, the stillness, warmth, and solitude that give those days their shape. And when the males are off exploring I move back and forth between two lures: the lovely golden day that I sit and admire, and the camp. It awakens in me an unsuspected Swiss Family Robinson urge to constantly improve it out of bits of wood, flat stones, and string.

As I grow older, camping in remote areas becomes more of a need than a diversion. Why this is so I do not know, unless it is the enormous relief of being out of the human current if only briefly. The ancient terror of being small, lost in a hostile vastness, is now replaced with a sense of the blessedness of this same smallness. It persuades us that since the landscape shows no signs of man, his greed and ingenuity are perhaps not as pervasive as they seem and, reprieved, we can slip back into the natural world from which our clever brains have driven us. Under the lightening sky I open my eyes to each new day, stretch, and almost say aloud in the coolness of the silver dawn: Good morning, world.

In the hands of a zoologist camping goes by another name, the field trip, but although the emphasis is different, the essential ingredients of cooking over a wood fire and sleeping on the ground are still there. I remember a pickup truck that appeared at our back door some years ago. It was filled with cages of fish-eating bats and buckets of ripe fish. Out of the cab stepped a University of California zoologist and his wife, he brimming with satisfaction at the tangible and hideously visible and stinking results of his field trip to the west coast of Mexico, and she radiating the tanned good health of days spent camping on shining sands and swimming in a sparkling ocean.

It was still in the first year of our marriage that I went on my first herpetological camping trip. Early spring rains had softened the desert with misty swatches of new green, and bright flowers nodded among the rocks and cactus. Bill hoped that the renewed warmth had also enticed the reptiles out of their winter holes, so we headed for an isolated canyon in the solemn mountains to the south. At their feet we turned onto a dirt road along which we bounced for several miles until we came to a rotting gate half off its hinges, beside which sprawled a large dead horse. While our attention was still riveted to this Caldwellian scene, three hefty bearded men rode around the corner of a nearby shack. Bill rolled down the car window, allowing the full-bodied aroma of the decaying horse to drift in. He leaned out and asked the men:

"Could you tell me where Montosa Canyon is?"

"Yeah," answered the biggest and burliest. "It's the next canyon to the south. Ain't huntin' are ya? That's part of our range over there an' we don't like nobody hangin' around." The three, slouched in their saddles, with guns at their hips in the best western cinema tradition, surveyed us suspiciously.

"Oh, no!" Bill hastened to assure them, "I'm a student from the University and I'm after snakes. Sure would appreciate it if you would give us permission to camp there a few days." After a brief silence while all three stared at Bill, the spokesman shoved his sweat-stained hat to the back of his head and scratched.

"Well, now. Snakes, ya say? D'ya eat 'em?"

"No, I'm a zoologist and we catch them for study. Do you have many around here?"

"Sure do, mostly them rattlers. There's a big one hangin' over the fence yonder, if the buzzards ain't et 'im. Shot 'im a couple days ago. Ye can have 'im if ya want."

"Thank you very much," said Bill, "but we can only use them alive. We're mostly after the smaller, rarer snakes."

"Well, go ahead, young fella. But be sure an' close the gates." With that they rode off shaking their heads, and we hastily retreated before they changed their minds. They marked the beginning of a long line of characters and rugged individualists that we were to meet in the backwashes of Arizona's mountains and canyons.

We later learned more about those gentlemen: how they appeared on the border scene many years ago when mostly Mexicans were ranching in the area and, posing as greenhorns, made themselves the butt of the jokes and laughter during roundups by their clumsy and unavailing attempts to rope a calf. However, when no one was looking, they roped any unmarked calves neatly enough and branded them for their own. So their herds grew. One of the brothers, whose temper was quicker than his trigger finger, ended with a forty-five slug in his head.

Under a spreading mesquite tree we "made camp," which consisted of throwing together a few stones for the fireplace, gathering wood, and spreading out our sleeping bags on a tarp. Recently I was asked if I were not afraid to sleep on the ground, what with all those snakes and bugs wandering around. For some reason I had never thought of it. Had I voiced such a fear to Bill, he undoubtedly would have thought of no more perfect way to be awakened than by a rare specimen slithering across him, and giving him a little time, he might even have devised a way to attract them.

While the fire burned down to coals we set off to investigate the area around camp by turning over rocks and logs and poking into mounds of decaying cactus. Here is a new world to the novice, the multitude of life under things. Beneath my first rock was a colony of those many-legged gray armadillo-like bugs that come to life in the sudden daylight, those that I always call bug-bugs, but which are commonly called pill bugs. Beneath the second I found nothing, but under the third a scorpion was resting. On being disturbed, he instantly raised his tail, stinger at the ready. So must have looked that fantastically adventurous first scorpion as he crawled out of the Silurian sea onto dry rock, the first animal to try a new life in the air. For millions of years he has crawled about, unchanged and unchanging, indiscriminately lifting his tail in warning to *Tyrannosaurus rex, Eohippus,* mastodon, and man. Nonchalantly and unimpressed, he watches them come and go, confident of his successful adaptation to survival that has guaranteed him such permanence.

My second desert camping trip included our six-months-old son. With barely a moment's hesitation I bundled the baby and a minimum of his paraphernalia into the borrowed truck and we were off to pick up a rare vine snake from an old prospector who lived in a canyon near an abandoned mining town. By then I had decided that two possible courses of action were open to me: I could either stay behind and feel sorry for myself, or go along. I have always chosen the second, and though it may result in anything from bliss to exhaustion, I have learned never to complain, for there is one irrefutable answer: "But dear, you didn't *have* to come!"

We arrived at the prospector's shack just after lunch. While Bill was out collecting and our son was napping in the back of the truck, I listened to the prospector tell of the days when he had been in the Alaska gold rush of '98 and how later in this very cabin he had stood off a band of marauding Yaquis. As I sat on a stump he had courteously placed for me by his open door, I couldn't help wishing that my Eastern college classmates could see me now, off in the wilds of the desert, with a real prospector beside me spinning tales of gold and Indians. I wondered at the loneliness and privations of such a life, and I envied the rare affinity he enjoyed with the natural world around him.

Next, we fell under the spell of the strange shifting margin where the desert meets the sea. They are kindred spirits, the desert and the sea, one as unrelenting as the other. For hundreds of miles along both sides of the Gulf of California each marches out of an inner silence to lap at the other, and on hundreds of deserted beaches they mingle their sands. In some places the desert brings down almost to the water's edge weird fleshy plants covered with thorns, in others it spills great dark boulders into the ocean itself. The sea, not to be outdone, lines its lip with rainbow shells and seaweed, but its most exotic wares it displays in tide pools. Like a child at a country fair, the passer-by wanders along, dazzled by the attractions on either hand.

First he peers down into the clear water of a small pool where purple sea urchins and spidery starfish are silhouetted against the bottom. He watches the turquoise sea anemones wave their tentacles, the long red worms ooze out from under a rock, a tiny octopus retreat into a crevice. Turning his back on this fantastic world, he walks into another, picking up a conch and two sand dollars on his way, until he reaches a boojum tree, and in its sliver of shade he sits.

In the foreign element of water we expect to find queer things; it is when they dare to sprout in the familiar air that we are properly amazed. Quite simply, the boojum is the queerest. Long known from Baja California where it is called "cirio," meaning candle, it was discovered in Sonora, Mexico, some years ago by Godfrey Sykes of the Desert Laboratory in Tucson, who stared at it and said, remembering *The Hunting of the Snark*, "Ho, ho, a boojum, definitely a boojum." This huge, elongated, upside-down carrot could well illustrate Lewis Carroll's odd creature that lived on distant desert shores. A relative of the ocotillo, it bears no resemblance to it except in the leaves that cover the

Cirios, or "boojums," Baja California

short bristly branches sticking out here and there along the fleshy trunk, which sometimes grows as high as sixty feet.

Driving back and forth between Tucson and the Gulf, we kept noticing an extensive black mountain mass to the west, known generally as the Pinacate. This lava field proved to be the most singular of all the places where we have camped. When Bill wished to install an exhibit at the Museum illustrating color adaptation in reptiles, he decided that the Pinacates, where he had heard tales of black lizards, would be an appropriate place to collect the necessary specimens darker in color than their brothers of the nearby sandy deserts. We therefore planned a field trip to this area, and in due course set out one early spring morning in a caravan of four jeeps for what has been called "the devil's backyard."

At that time we could find out so little about this lava region that our projected trip was to be as much one of exploration as of herpetology, and this new aspect filled me with romantic conjecture ". . . like stout Cortez when with eagle eyes / He star'd at the Pacific—and all his men / Look'd at each other with a wild surmise . . ." A gap of two hundred years stretches between the accounts of the adventurous and hardy Spanish priests who first climbed the lava mountains, which they called Santa Clara, at the turn of the eighteenth century, and the only two modern accounts. The Spanish priests were interested in this barren spot not only because they hoped to baptize whatever Indian souls were living in so unpromising a land, but also because they wished to climb the highest peak in an attempt to determine whether California, visible across the narrow sea, was an island or a peninsula, a geographic puzzle discussed even in the drawing rooms of Europe. The current popular theory was that this sea was a strait, similar to the strait of Gibraltar, and California was a series of islands that finally connected with the Marianas and Japan. But from what he saw from Pinacate Peak, Father Kino, the most famous of the Spanish priests, was convinced that the

Typical sharp-rising desert mountains, near the Camino del Diablo

sea ended not many miles to the north. Though others still disagreed with him, man's curiosity in the area dwindled, and it lay dormant until the modern age of exploration.

Of the two modern accounts, William T. Hornaday's *Camp-Fires on Desert and Lava* is perhaps the more detailed, though we found ourselves using the maps appearing in his book with no more ease than those appearing in *New Trails in Mexico*, by Carl Lumholtz, published a few years later. Hornaday wished to explore this unknown territory and study the flora and fauna, especially the mountain sheep rumored to be scrambling around the dead volcanoes. While there, he collected two prong-horned antelope and seven mountain sheep (bighorns) for the Carnegie Museum.

Armed with these accounts and their respective maps as well as with those of the Spanish padres, we set out confidently. The two most important problems facing us that first day were whether we would find a way to get the jeeps in over the lava flows that spread out from the center mountain mass and whether we would find the tanks or water holes rumored to be somewhere about. We decided to follow Hornaday's route and to come into the area from the north, so at the Mexican border we turned west onto the highway that goes to Tijuana. All around us stretched the terrible *gran desierto*, the *mal país*. Close to where we now drove comfortably and quickly, covered wagons and travelers on horseback had once inched achingly along, for this was one of the routes to fabled California and gold. So many died of thirst on the way that the early road earned the name of Camino del Diablo. In the official report of the United States section of the International Boundary Commission's surveyors who journeyed through this country in the 1890's, appeared this description:

Mile after mile the journey stretches through this land of "silence, solitude and sunshine," with little to distract the eye from the awful surrounding dreariness and desolation except the bleaching skeletons of horses and the painfully frequent crosses which mark the graves of those who perished of thirst . . . in a single day's ride 65 of these graves were counted by the roadside, one containing an entire family.

The Pinacates, looming darkly on our left, started us looking for tracks. After several false starts on trails that petered out, we found a more substantial one that headed in the right direction. It had been covered with cotton seeds, which gave a surprisingly firm surface in the sifting sandy soil. This road dwindled at a deserted homestead but continued on faintly towards the lava mountains, winding in and out of an ocotillo forest whose long tentacle stems, green with leaves, waved slowly in the wind like seaweed in a gentle current.

We were able to locate ourselves on Hornaday's map and therefore knew when we had come to MacDougal Pass, named after the head of the Desert Laboratory, who was a member of the expedition. We lined up our jeeps where the horses of the Hornaday expedition had lined up fifty years ago, and commemorated our event as had his photographer. Holding his picture before us, we could pick out the very same saguaros and note the amount of growth over the years. Accompanying us, to add yet another link to the past, was the son of Godfrey Sykes, who went with Hornaday to map the area for his book.

Before long a smooth low ridge lay on our right like the hump of a sleeping whale, and on reaching its crest our first crater abruptly and terrifyingly burst open at our feet. This gigantic hole in the ground was not at all what I expected, as I had always thought of a crater as a mountain with its top blown off. Yet it is amply, overwhelmingly spectacular: about four-hundred feet deep and three-quarters of a mile across to the other side. From our feet the rim sloped steeply to precipitous cliffs which dropped down in layers of basalt and cinder beds, ending in a talus slope of debris that slanted to the bottom.

Our geologist informed us that undoubtedly this crater, and the other seven or so like it to be found here, began with a series of violent gas explosions which forced a passageway, or conduit, upwards through the overlying rocks to the surface from an underlying chamber of molten rock. Succeeding gas blasts probably enlarged the conduit as chunks of material were torn from the walls by hurtling rock fragments in the gas column.

Geologists differ somewhat in their concept of the next stage as to exactly how these great holes were formed. However, it is generally agreed that the uprushing gas deposited a cone of volcanic debris, and then when the pressure was exhausted from the underground chamber, its roof collapsed and all but the outer edge of the cone fell into the void. Recent evidence also indicates that the floor of one of these craters was a Pleistocene lake.

Beyond MacDougal Crater were three small craters in the shape of a clover leaf, surrounded by a common rim. Towards late afternoon we made camp at Papago Tanks, spreading out our sleeping bags in an open flat area hedged by palo verde and mesquite. Close to our campsite was a small, narrow, steep-sided canyon whose bottom was stepped with several smooth basins. These successfully caught and held rainwater for months, thus providing the wildlife with a miraculous drink. The Sand Papago Indians used to camp here, hence the name.

These nomadic people, never numbering more than a few hundred, wandered in family groups over this pitiless land in

Papago Tanks

search of food. Juan Mateo Manje, a Spanish soldier accompanying Father Kino, described a group of the Indians they saw here in 1701 as "poor naked people, who sustain themselves by roots, locusts, and lizards, which they call iguanas, and some fish. All these Indians were instructed in the Word of God." To catch these fish they would have had to cross the great band of sand dunes that lie between the Pinacate and the Gulf of California.

A rancher by the name of Thomas Childs, living along the border towards the close of the nineteenth century, spoke of these Indians in hardly more flattering terms, recounting how they wore their hair long and how "at times they would plaster it all with mud. That was to kill the lice." At this time the Mexican government was busily rounding up these Indians and moving them to other parts, as they had been plundering the wagon trains of immigrants and killing them as they struggled along the Camino del Diablo. According to Childs the Indians were after the white man's tobacco, for which they had an irresistible craving. Smoking had its drawbacks even in those days.

In the canyon itself the sun glinted blindingly off the lava where it had been polished by centuries of water and gravel rushing by after infrequent rains. Considering the hardness of the lava and the rarity of such scouring floods, it was a mystery how such a slickness could ever have been achieved. Wild flowers and tiny shrubs, grateful for any moisture, grew out of the cracks or around the edges of the pools. Above one shrub with gray-green leaves and clusters of lavender flowers hovered a red-throated hummingbird. What was my surprise on crushing the flower between my fingers to smell the delicate sweet odor of English lavender. Equally incongruous to the bleak jumble of surrounding black rock were the fragile, almost transparent, fairy shrimp swimming in a pocket of water. In a flat rock above one of the pools a more energetic member of the party found a series of holes where the Indians used to grind their seeds.

It was a pleasant place to sit after a day of jouncing in a jeep, with one's feet in a clear pool of water, a few lone sentinel saguaros against the skyline, the doves whirring in from the desert in a frenzy of excitement to drink among the reflections of lava walls, and no sound but the whisper of the wind against bare rock and the calls of the resting birds.

Our goal the next morning was Sykes Crater, said to be the most spectacular of them all. It was a stiff climb up the steep sides covered with loose rubble, and a hot one even under a March sun. For those who were collecting specimens of glassy feldspar and spindle-shaped volcanic bombs, it was harder still as their bags became heavier and heavier. The occasional pieces of grayish-white granite that dotted the slope looked out of place among the black debris, but our geologist said they were quite to be expected,

Camp under the palo verde at Papago Tanks

Elegante Crater in the Pinacate

having been gouged out of the walls of the passageway deep in the
earth through which the stream of gas was rushing. The vegetation was extremely sparse: ocotillo, creosote, limber-bush (also
called Sangre-de-Christo because of the reddish sap of its roots),
small nondescript gray shrubs, and suddenly a four-foot elephant
tree. These pinky, fleshy-trunked trees are common farther south,
there growing much larger, but this was the first one I had ever
seen. It reminded me again what a curious land it was that I was
visiting.

A more spellbinding sight cannot easily be imagined than
that which greeted us on reaching the crater's lip. Even the rap-
turous account in Hornaday's book had not properly prepared us
for the three-mile-around hole 750 feet deep. The wind, blowing

strongly across the crater top, put the ocotillo into a wild dance and threatened to send us whirling down into that magnificent abyss. Standing there we felt the same awe as had Juan Manje two hundred years before when he looked into "a big hole of such depth that it caused terror and fear." Curiously, Father Kino did not describe it; those early rugged gentlemen took the most amazing things quite in their stride, and they briskly covered between breakfast and lunch what for us would be a major undertaking requiring days of planning and mounds of equipment.

We sat on the crater's edge, enveloped by an enormous windy solitude. On one side the sooty volcanic ground slipped down to the circle of high cliffs that formed the sides of the colossal pit. They shone red in the sun except where they inked-in a black shadow on the distant sandy floor. I expected to see prehistoric monsters, in good comic book style, come lumbering out of the darkness and lock in mortal combat. Perched far above them, I would hear their terrible cries and watch them struggle until the clouds of dust hid them from view. But today, scattered on that remote arena were only a few saguaros looking like soldier matchsticks lined up by a child about to play a game of war.

On the other side stretched a sea of lava, a bleak biblical wilderness, a nakedness too harsh for sensibilities. Yet its awful splendor commanded me to look and to admire. In one direction rose the frowning central mountain mass, misty and mysterious, with its great black lava skirt spread out to dry. Most of this lava had leaked out of cracks in the mountain's flanks, for the mountains themselves were older piles of basaltic lava flows, volcanic ash, and debris. Tree-lined arroyos, like pale green ribbons, wound faintly through the lava plains over which were dotted volcanic hills or cinder cones in various stages of erosion, some black, some reddish, some gray. From above, the plain looked deceptively smooth, and it is not until you come upon the edge of a flow or a canyon that you have any idea of the inherent turbulence of lava or of the ferocity of its jagged rocks and boulders.

In another direction sprawled a granite mountain range. Like a dying saurian, it lay on the lava, its rough cracked skin clinging to its emaciated frame so that every bone showed. Beyond it a second range lay almost buried in the sand, only its jagged crest protruding. Farther away still, stretched the miles of sand dunes that divide the lava fields from the Gulf, which we could just see shimmering in the distance.

Several years later I sat on the rim of another such crater on the other side of the peaks, watching through binoculars my husband, two sons, and two friends as they searched for a rumored trail. They, as I, were tasting the wilderness, each in his own fashion. Soon they disappeared behind a lava flow and I was alone. A steady wind blew, an effortless empty wind like the wind in high places. Perhaps this is what made me feel so close to the sun, as if the world were at my feet. Or was it because the black, antiseptic, desolate land above which I sat shone so clean, continually swept as it was by the wind?

Soft green meadows, sun-sprinkled woods, a stream idling through a summer day, are as welcoming as a mother's lap in which you can melt and elude yourself. But on the side of a black barren hill in the middle of an infinite emptiness your kittenish smiles are ignored with a great and unblinking indifference, as they would be ignored in the middle of an ocean. Here you have to meet yourself directly, not with mannered, self-analytical pickings, but in another realm—to be so quiet that you can feel all of a piece, sun-fused. And in the airy stillness you are like a hawk, sailing on the invisible currents of your being. Was there ever a content as wide as this?

On the way back to camp the scuttling of a horned toad caught my husband's eye. Quickly he grabbed it. Although a common species, it was of a most uncommon color. Centuries of living in a black world had changed its color to match, neatly illustrating the survival value of such camouflage.

The Buried Range, so named by Hornaday, fascinated us as it had fascinated him. Hornaday had predicted that it would be completely engulfed in another fifty years, yet now it appeared to us much as it did in his photograph. Being curious to see the range close at hand, we set off after lunch in its direction, our jeeps crawling on an even fainter track, over the lava plains fingered with arroyos and ridges that we had to struggle down into or up over; and always the cyclopean eye of the Pinacate peaks, blue in the afternoon haze, watched us. Some of the volcanic hills that we passed were dotted with pink fleshy limber-bush where seemingly nothing should be but bare bones. Creosote and brittle-bush, cholla and ocotillo also struggled to stay alive. That year's unusually wet spring had left its mark even here, and wild flowers were massed in open areas and along the arroyos: sore-eye poppies, thistles with large white blossoms, an occasional lily. Some of the palo verde were heavily shrouded with a small-leafed vine, and their resulting grotesque shapes contributed to the eeriness of an already eery landscape.

That night we camped on the very edge of the lava flow, as close to the sand dunes and the buried mountain range as we

The end of the Buried Range, with evening primroses in foreground

could safely get the jeeps. We were in the midst of a graveyard of palo verde and ironwood skeletons that cast contorted shadows in the low afternoon sun. Hang a few limp watches on their twisted branches and you would have a Dali painting. Every creosote grew out of a mound of sand, and the varied profusion of animal tracks leading into and out of holes or up and around sand hillocks provoked speculation. Here a lizard had scurried, there a kangaroo rat. A kit fox had rushed around that bush, a coyote had ambled past this hole, and over there a sidewinder had left its characteristic marks. It was a relief to contemplate this microcosm in the midst of such a flagrant opposite.

A lizard darted past me into a too-shallow hole. Unable to get his tail in all the way, he quickly reappeared and dashed off in search of larger accommodations. By my foot I noticed a minute sand pit at the bottom of which I could just see the ends of an ant lion's pinchers. This larva lives in wait for an ant to fall into his trap. The victim, unable to crawl up the sliding sand walls, is then seized and sucked dry. On this diet the aggressor matures and makes himself a silken cocoon in which to pupate. Eventually he flies off as a small drab version of the damselfly, quite unlike the fierce ant lion that he once was.

One track, more peculiar than the others, had us baffled, until we found at its end a large shiny black beetle, the kind that stands on its head when disturbed. Known commonly as the stink beetle, it is also known locally as the Pinacate beetle, "pinacate" being a corruption of the Aztec "pinacatl" meaning small ground beetle. It lent its name to this area either because of its abundance here, or perhaps because the central peaks could possibly be thought to bear some resemblance to this creature standing on its head. The Papago name of Tjuktóak, meaning Black Mountain, is more sensible if less pronounceable.

The trek the following day over the sand dunes to the buried range was weird, difficult, and very beautiful. Almost immediately we were swallowed up by the vast silent sea of shifting sand. After a few hours we came to the sand-covered sides of the mountains and clambered up to their rocky crests. We looked out across interminable heaving dunes that stretched westward as far as the eye could see. Great dunes, they were, some up to six hundred feet high, as we determined later by sonar altimeter. We wondered how many other mountains were perhaps buried under them.

No less strange than the dunes themselves is how they arrived here. Our geologist suggested an incredible but probable process: the Colorado River carrying its load of silt and sand gathered from the mountains of Utah, dropping it at its delta, the ocean washing away the silt and leaving the clean sand for the along-shore currents to move as far as here, a distance of sixty or seventy miles. The winds then helped to distribute the sand inland and to pile it into dunes. Or, in short, what once came from mountains is now burying mountains.

The walk back to camp in the late afternoon was even more spectacular, for the lowering sun brought to life endless patterns of light and shadow. We were all that moved, except for the faint plumes of sand blowing off the knife-edges of each dune, and the occasional fringe-toed lizard that darted out from under our feet to race wildly away and dive back into the sand when at a safe distance. In this sterile world of whispering sand, spring remarkably had also managed to leave its touch, and delicate white evening primroses bloomed in infrequent patches.

The following morning we decided to try and find another of the rumored tanks. For hours we bounced slowly along, pausing periodically to examine the country through binoculars in an attempt to match up the cinder cones with those described by Hornaday or illustrated in his pictures. Unexpectedly we came upon a spot where the lava crust was thin and had broken through into a large subterranean cave smelling strongly of bats. It reminded us of Lumholtz's account of going with an Indian guide to a similar cave near the Pinacate peaks. According to Indian legend, that cave was one of the main residences of their creator, the Elder Brother, called Íitoi (E'etoi). After a flood Íitoi "entered his cask which floated four times around the world and then he landed at Pinacate and was very thin after the long voyage." As the Papago Mount Ararat the Pinacates acquired even more mystery.

Legend also tells of a passage running from the cave westward under the mountains and sea, to end at an island where the Elder Brother's wife lived! The god was said to have less important houses in this region, and we wondered if this cave into which we were peering was one of them.

The track we were attempting to follow finally ended near the remains of a crater with a red cinder cone in the middle of it. In a small hollow nearby we discovered a large Indian olla probably used for storage and we left it undisturbed as a small memorial to those who had once lived here. Unfortunately, on our next trip when we returned to look at it, the olla was gone.

Sand Papago windbreak and a metate with grinding stone

After some effort we at last found a trail which, as it led away from the edge of the flow and towards the mountains, we hopefully concluded would take us to Tule Tank. So off we set, for the first time heading directly towards the Pinacate peaks themselves. The country grew increasingly rough, with deeper arroyos and higher ridges which really challenged the jeeps. Often what we seemed to be following was a sheep or Indian trail. Several were heading in what we thought was the right direction, for logically a water hole in such an arid region would be spoked with trails.

We came upon a stone-ringed place scattered with seashells. This must have been a stopping place of the Sand Papagos on their way to and from the ocean to catch fish and gather mollusks and salt. Apparently Papagos that lived much farther away would also come here for salt, as it was a valuable trade commodity.

At one of our frequent pauses to spread out and explore, one of us spotted a narrow canyon with a large deep pool at the base of sheer walls—Tule Tank, we deduced. So we made camp on a smooth patch of ground close to the canyon's edge. Nearby were the remains of a rude windbreak the Indians had made of rocks, all that they would ever bother to build in the way of shelter. A broken metate lay to one side, as well as quantities of pottery shards and obsidian flakes. The primitive Sand Papagos made no pottery themselves, but they traded for it from more industrious tribes like the Yumas. As hard as we looked we found no arrowheads. Perhaps it takes boy eyes, for when we brought our sons, they found over half a dozen beautiful ones made of obsidian, plus decorated pottery and several stone grinders.

Tule was also zoologically lucrative. Someone found a hummingbird's nest, another a tree lizard impaled on an ocotillo thorn by a shrike in order to guarantee himself a convenient future meal, and another a particularly large many-headed barrel cactus, this one with over three hundred heads. Around its base and protected by the spines were the doorways to a number of rodent burrows.

This was as isolated a spot as I had ever been in. Civilization seemed to be eons away. We were travelers suspended in time, and the movements that we made as we cooked supper marked our existence as faintly as the lines left on the sand by a scurrying lizard. And our voices were absorbed into the darkening sky along with those of the yapping coyote and the sleepy birds.

On our last day we awoke to find ourselves in the midst of a sand storm, which hurried our departure. Not only ourselves, but the entire landscape, or what we could see of it, was coated with sand, and the slumbering volcanoes retreated behind a brown, impenetrable curtain. By the end of the day we were once again on an asphalt highway where cars were rushing to the next semblance of civilization. We could imagine the occupants glancing apprehensively out at the surrounding desolation. Behind the blowing sand the Pinacates returned once more to their accustomed solitude.

But our appetites had been whetted, and the Pinacates draw us back to them almost every spring. One year we saw mountain sheep, one year two bands of prong-horned antelope, one year the prayer sticks in the sacred cave, and one year at Papago Tanks we met Alberto Celaya, who guided Lumholtz into this region in 1910. Around the campfire he told us of visiting the last of the resident Sand Papagos who was living there under the same palo verde tree where we were sitting. Every spring, with "wild surmise" we scramble over the black lava wastes and gaze down into yet another terrible abyss, or perhaps the ruins of an Indian village. The first year that we took our sons, one of them said as we approached the Pinacates, "Mexico is sure lucky, it's so rich in lava." He paused, then added, "But when will the volcanoes interrupt?"

Wolf spider, showing six of his eight eyes

10

Night

THE desert at night is yet a different place. To walk in it by the light of the moon is to palpate a different kind of reality with different senses. Ears take precedence over eyes, and skin takes precedence over ears. You begin to "feel" in a way that you never do by day. Against bare arms, against bare legs, the summer night rubs itself as does a cat, and newly awakened hands stroke it softly. The two-tone world blurs one's own identity and so one is absorbed more easily into the surroundings. Strangely, I feel much more a part of the desert at night than I do in the day.

The summer nights are the most winning. After the immolating heat of the day, they beguile one with their cool gentleness. We, as well as the animals, crawl out of our holes and wander about. In the moonlight the ground is white; the shrubs and cacti dissolve into nondescript grayness so that only their hard black shadows have substance, and I instinctively skirt them as if they are actual forms against which I might bruise a shin. The mountains too are gray, mottled with queer black patches that the bright moonlight makes the ridges cast. As the sunlight here is brighter than in other places, so too is the moonlight, and the old story that you can read a newspaper by it is quite true. The night is like a negative where the normal order is reversed and I am disoriented and yet at home.

The immobile desert does not fool me now, for the night air

ripples with tiny sounds that disclose its secret life. My ear cannot identify them, but the presence of the nameless creatures is reassuring nonetheless. We almost always end down by the stream, and if it is running, we walk along its bank. The round moon is as precise in the dark still water as in the dark still sky. We follow it downstream, losing it in the rush of water, catching it in the pools. And where the water runs over the rocks, we watch the moonlit bubbles like minute boats swarm up, scatter, and flicker out.

We sit on a log looking at the water. Close by, a water bug skates across the face of the moon, pulling it out behind him like a golden spring, until it suddenly snaps back, quivers, and again is whole. A small animal scurries by through the bushes, a bat flitters by overhead, a toad jumps with a plop into a pool. Behind its placid countenance the night is restless; like a black bag, it jerks as unseen forces stir. As we walk back to the house a screech owl drops his tumbling trill into the darkness, and momentarily we are hypnotized by the magic of that sound.

Sometimes I am asked by a newcomer who arrives at our house and looks around, puzzled, "But you're so far away from everything. Don't you get lonely living out here by yourselves?" Then I think of our summer nights full of the sound of other lives being lived close by, and I am reminded of an incident in a book about the Congo pigmies. One moonlit night the author, who was living with these forest people, came upon one of them dancing alone and singing as he looked up at the treetops. To the question of why he was dancing there alone, the pigmy answered, "But I'm not dancing alone, I'm dancing with the forest, dancing with the moon."

Into our house the summer night drifts on a waft of cool air, on a coyote's cry, and we stir in our sleep. At night the evening primroses bloom, the mesquite leaves close up, the owls hunt on silent wings, the coons fish in our stream. At night the kangaroo rats hop about on long springy legs, gathering seeds, and the rattlesnakes ooze over the ground in search of them, moving in a peculiarly straight, unwiggling line that gives them a sinister purposefulness. And the giant desert centipede in leg wavelets hunts for something smaller than himself on which to make his dinner.

At night a friend of ours claims he can hear the termites chewing on his house. Unfortunately I have never heard them, hard as I have listened, but twice in our own house I have found tunnels of the subterranean species, glued to the adobe wall, leading from their nests in the ground up to a wooden sill. And not long ago we noticed the small pole supporting our telephone wire listing dangerously, a sure sign that termites have been at work.

Nothing is sneakier than a termite. With what complacency man sits in his house looking out at the somnolent and excluded desert, and all the while its vanguards are chewing away at the foundations. Man has generously provided the termite with appetizing meals ranging from posts to tasty houses, and they need no other invitation to begin eating them than, like the mountains to the climber, the fact that they are there. Until the pest-control man appears, a man's house makes a far more agreeable environment for them than their natural habitat of dead trees and saguaros, where they are less well protected from their deadly enemy the ant and are much more likely to eat themselves out of house and home. Oddly enough they cannot digest their cellulose meals without help, and so in their digestive tracts colonies of one-celled protozoa live who break down the cellulose into a form of nourishment that the termite can assimilate.

Not all of our Arizona termites—and we have about twenty species here—use our houses only at mealtimes. A clever kind, as he eats, excavates new galleries and rooms in which to live, a system that to me seems brilliantly economic. This dry-wood termite is particularly well adapted to desert living by having an outer "skin" that contains a waxy substance which minimizes dehydration, much as do the resinous leaves of the creosote. He is able to survive for months without free water, and though he will shrink under these conditions, when the rain wets the wood, he will quickly swell back to normal size. It would seem logical that these termites can also manufacture their own water internally as does the kangaroo rat.

As eager as I am to eliminate them from the premises, I find termites fascinating, and I am contemplating installing my own personal colony in a series of flat glass containers interconnected by tubes, as has a University of Arizona professor, so that I too can spy on them. The other evening I peered at a damp-wood termite through a dissecting scope, and on close scrutiny he turned out to be a very handsome animal, of shiny white alabaster body-sections and a round head that sprouted two long feelers of tiny amber beads.

Though occupying one of the lowest rungs of the insect ladder, their highly organized life can hold its own with even that of the ant, so that they have earned the name of "white ant." Happily they have several important differences that in my opinion places them above the ant. The termite workers are both male and female, while those of the ant (and bee and wasp) are always female. Perhaps I am predisposed in their favor because of their sexual democracy, though heaven knows I'm no feminist. Another difference is that besides a queen they also have a king. These two mate for life and live together in a royal chamber, enjoying a connubial bliss that may last as long as fifteen years. There they are carefully fed and tended by their loyal workers. Unlike the ant, the termite royalty is replaceable should disaster strike, thus ensuring the continuation of the colony.

Most of the workers are doomed to living out their lives in sexual immaturity. However, once a year, usually in the summer, a certain lucky number of them develop wings and are then potential queens or kings. When the weather conditions are right they swarm, scatter, and after dropping to the ground, lose their wings, pair off, burrow into wood, mate, and so begin a new colony. Fortunately for our houses, most of them fall prey to birds, lizards, ants, and other insects that rush to the scene to gorge themselves.

Another lucky few grow into soldiers. These privileged members of the colony have enlarged armored heads and enormous pinchers which impede their ability to eat in the usual termite manner, so they have to be fed by the workers. The workers are obliging creatures who not only feed them but also groom them, and sometimes, in a glass-contained colony, you will see a soldier stretched out like a sybaritic Roman in obvious bliss while he is rubbed and patted. The soldiers sound the alarm by knocking their heads against the wood or clicking their jaws, which, termites being deaf, produces a detectable vibration. One kind of soldier has a head so shaped that with it he can block a tunnel entrance in the face of an intruder.

Power never liking to be threatened, the reigning monarchs and soldiers secrete a substance that is circulated throughout the colony by the feeding and grooming processes which suppresses the sexual maturing of the workers. But a certain number always manage to escape this chemically induced bondage so that the proportion of soldiers is kept constant, and come summer, a plentiful supply of winged ones is ready to swarm.

Not long ago our nine-year-old was writing a report on the social insects and asked, "Is the termite a sociable insect?" And indeed he is, for he prefers living with us to living without us, a dubious compliment.

*　　*　　*

Again it is fall. The summer rain clouds have vanished, leaving behind them a running stream, grass, and a calm, unmarked sky. The days are still warm, but the morning and evening shadows are tinged with cold. The white-wings have gone, soon the buzzards will be flying south, and most of the reptiles will be looking for winter resting places.

In the boys' rooms snakes curl up in corners of glass cages. Never have the boys found so many. Peter has a gopher snake, John two kingsnakes, a spotted night snake, and a patch-nose, Mike a large black racer, and Hugh a garter snake. He greets every guest hopefully with "Would you like to see my gardener snake?" and if the answer is in the affirmative he goes proudly off, leading his victim by the hand. But our snake population is a fluctuating one, for always at least one has temporarily escaped. They disappear and reappear disconcertingly, and just the other day I found Peter's gopher snake asleep in a mislaid slipper.

Some months ago seven Mexican wolves were born at the Museum, too many for the mother to care for comfortably, so I offered to take over one whom we called Beowulf. I learned how to give him his bottle and the other tricks to being a wolf mother, such as providing comforting bare feet for him to sleep between while I wrote. He quickly grew into a long-legged, large-footed gangling puppy, who looked a little like a German shepherd but with a much larger head, more nervous active ears, and a remarkable elasticity that allowed him to turn spectacular somersaults as he romped with our patient dog. At first she tried to teach him to play with sticks, but he preferred her tail, my old sandal, a ragged teddy bear of the boys' that he shook alarmingly, and anything else that he could find.

Now he is a willful, bushy-tailed adolescent of formidable energy and bounce. In fact, like Christopher Robin's friend, Tigger, he seems a great deal bigger because of his bounces, and goodness knows he is big enough without them. On my return after even a short absence, he charges up to welcome me with a doggish enthusiasm that literally takes my breath away. When I finally manage to struggle out of the car I feel quite as anxious as Piglet being greeted by Tigger, that "Very Bouncy Animal, with a way of saying How-do-you-do which always left your ears full of sand, even after Kanga had said, 'Gently, Tigger dear,' and had helped you up again." I have said "Gently, dear Wolfy!" many times, and other things besides, with no better results.

Our front entrance looks like a junk yard, or is it a wolf den? Bits of old shoes, bones, rags, paper, and other undefinable matter are scattered over the gravel. After he had flattened the flower-beds in the west patio and chewed off the vines, in desperation I decided to keep him out so that my eyes could rest on at least one decent "unwolfed" spot. The minute I locked the gate in his face, a grave tactical error, he set himself to getting inside, and in exactly five seconds he had climbed over the gate. Matching wits with a wolf, should one be foolish enough to attempt it, takes total concentration. No sooner had I built an extension to the gate than he was over the wall. Not having enough lumber on hand to build a barricade seven or eight feet high, I fastened cholla joints every few inches along the top of the wall. It took just one brush

Beowulf and I

with the cholla to persuade him that for the time being he did not really want to get inside. Our new housekeeper has had to move the clothesline inside that patio, as his laundry-day entertainment is pulling the wash off the line. Fortunately she is ingenious as well as resilient and undaunted, neither wolves nor bobcats upsetting her in the least.

Now when I look out the window my eyes rest victoriously on once-again respectable flowerbeds over which hang long lines of socks and shirts stirring gently in the breeze. Beyond the gate Beowulf sits craning his neck and grinning at me, and a flicker of doubt assails me. I find myself shouting at him, "Well, my friend, who cares about the socks! I counted six new buds on the gardenia bush."

Even should one manage a stout sense of victory in the face of sock-bedecked flowerbeds and a wolf's grin, sadly it will be short-lived, for his roving eye will soon discover the next inevitable chink. A few days ago I went to arrange the guest house in the

Peter and the wolf

The boys and Beowulf

wake of a departing friend, and the havoc spread before me was of hurricane proportions. Tangled on the floor were sheets, blankets, books, and towels, all generously sprinkled with the feathers from three pillows. A short time before, Beowulf, sitting innocently outside with seemingly nothing more on his mind than the sunshine and the view, must have noticed that our guest had not completely shut the door; and while we were busy with farewells, he ripped a large hole in the screen, pushed his way inside, and set to work. Whenever I scold him, he looks at me whimsically, his forehead slightly ruffled, and I can almost hear him say, "But you know, I'm just a pup."

How the boys manage him is a mystery, for he is rapidly becoming as big, strong, and stubborn as they. When they're playing badminton and he runs off with the bird, when he grabs whatever they're carrying and chews it up, when they're trying to

crawl through a newly completed tunnel through which he also is trying to crawl but from the other end, then tempers run a little short and I hear the sounds of battle. However, all is soon tranquil, nothing and no one is missing, and the game goes on. I have noticed, though, that if Beowulf becomes too pestiferous, our dog will rush up to divert him, an absolutely vital procedure if one is to carry anything safely from the car into the house.

Also in residence at the moment is a friend's bobkitten called Dangerous Dan McGrew, a coiled spring of a creature that never unwinds. I overheard Peter describing the new arrival to his grandmother: "He's little, he's cute, he's friendly, and he bites all the time." None of these statements are in the least conflicting, for both Peter and McGrew consider the bites to be amiable.

One evening when they were still very young, we had Beowulf, McGrew, and a visiting badger of approximately the same age all together in the study. The badger immediately went under the desk, where he caught and ate a beetle. On his reappearance the bobcat jumped him, which the badger completely ignored, so in disgust the bobcat jumped the wolf, who fell in a heap and rolled over. The badger then found himself a plastic dish to play with and pushed it off to a solitary corner where he spent the rest of the evening chewing it, pawing it, and generally rattling it noisily on the cement floor.

The bobcat and wolf, more convivial creatures, tumbled together this way and that, pausing only long enough to go over and inspect the badger periodically, who wouldn't so much as give them a sniff or glance. While the bobcat scrambled around the back of the couch in a fit of exuberance, the wolf climbed awkwardly in and out of the chair rungs like a child in a jungle gym, which performance the bobcat interrupted by leaping onto the chair seat and reaching down to slap the wolf with his paw. And then they both went off together to chew on the rug and take a nap.

Now, when I go outside, Beowulf bounds up and gives me

the traditional wolf greeting, a friendly shove with his shoulder, which at last I've learned to brace myself for, and grabs my leg with lengthening canines, his tail wagging. Like a coyote, he expresses his affection by grasping your most available appendage in his jaws. I try to remember that he does not like meat, much preferring dried dog food, egg, and cottage cheese. Then he flops over to have his belly rubbed. It is difficult to sort it all out. When I look into his wide-set yellow eyes as he chews my arm, I wonder if he knows he's a wolf. In the evening I listen to him howl, during the day I watch his eager, effortless lope, and I for one think of forests, plains and snowy nights.

When I go inside, McGrew makes a flying tackle out from under a chair and also grabs my leg. He is around the room like a whirling dervish, ricocheting off chairs, tables, and humans with equal impartiality. In moments of weakness we allow him into the study, where he quickly settles down to a figure eight flight pattern: floor to my desk-top, around my neck to the couch to Bill's desk-top, around his neck and back to the floor. I have to sit with my bare feet in the wastebasket so he can't chew my toes. After scattering Bill's papers for the sixth time, his exercise period comes to an abrupt end as he is removed to another part of the house.

Tiger Balm resents these intrusions of wolf and bobkitten. Whenever she sees them she growls, hisses, and walks stiff-legged with her ruff straight out and her short tail twitching.

A few nights ago I sat on the bank of the stream while Bill was chasing cows, his pet grievance, off the property. Beowulf, momentarily tired of exploring the night smells, came to sit close by me, and together we watched the moon shadows, our minds pursuing private pathways. And while we sat shoulder to shoulder, I thought about this strange thing, a wolf and a woman side by side, with the bittersweet awareness of our kinship and our difference. Unlike a dog who is bred to sit, his freely given companionship stirs within me a longing for something no longer known, something buried and unnoticed in our mindless cells.

This morning I saw our new substitute milkman reading the typed list of instructions tacked to the kitchen wall:

1. Beowulf the wolf: feed twice daily
   1 cup dog meal
   ½ can dog food
   1 egg yolk morning, cottage cheese evening
   1 vitamin pill
2. McGrew the bobkitten: feed 3X daily
   ½ pound horsemeat for the day mixed with 1 egg yolk, cottage cheese & 1 vitamin pill
3. Tiger Balm the bobcat: feed twice daily
   ½ pound horsemeat
   1 vitamin pill
4. Charley the parakeet
   every other day change water & refill seed dish
5. Tobermory the cat: feed when he wishes
   alternate canned liver & kidney
6. Nandy the dog: feed evening
   ½ can dog food
   1 cup dog meal
   4 yeast tablets
7. Peco the horse: feed twice daily
   1 bucket alfalfa pellets
8. Legs the tarantula
   keep water in dish filled
   feed a cricket or grasshopper once a week

IN CASE OF RATTLESNAKE BITE
   Use suction immediately and apply ice packs
   Call Dr. H. P. Limbacher—793–9311

He looked at me without a word and went out the door. A second later he reopened the door and asked, "Do you have much trouble getting a baby-sitter?"

The two younger boys and I spent this afternoon down by the stream. While I daydreamed in the hammock, the boys sat cross-legged in a small plastic boat, propelling themselves about with their hands. Tiring of this, they dropped the stone anchor mid-stream and talked idly in the sun, their voices blending with the insect hum. Every so often they dipped their fingers into the water to grab at a beetle or a tadpole. Their presence gave another dimension to the scene, like a painting brought to life by a figure placed in it. Without them the tableau before my eyes would have been flat; with them it was in the round, complete. That this should be so must mean more than I care to admit.

Later, having been forced by one animal or another to abandon whatever chair I was attempting to sit in, in order to read a book, I began mumbling about the dreadfulness of it all and how I was going to build a wolf-bobcat-boy-proof cage large enough to accommodate a chaise longue, a music box, and me in a feather boa, and there I would stay with the cage door locked from the inside. Bill, who overheard me, said sympathetically, "We *could* get rid of them all and start over again—with snails."

But at night our kingdom is peaceable and my feet are serenely planted in both worlds. Behind one bedroom door Beowulf

Toby and Tiger Balm

sighs in his sleep and curls himself tighter on his rug. Behind another I can hear Tiger Balm chasing her rubber ball. The boys burrow deeper in their beds, oblivious to the faint stirrings of their snakes out feeling the air with nervous tongues. In their bathroom McGrew is undoubtedly splashing in the toilet, whose lid they have forgotten to close. In the playroom the dog and cat dream on couch and chair. Through the open window come the sounds of the other world outside, and we are not alone.

11

Survival

A FEW months ago Peter, our oldest, and three friends of his took an overnight hike up into the mountains. They swam in the stream beside which they climbed, cooked their dinner over a fire, woke up in the night to watch the stars, and with dawn, relished the excitement of being alone on a mountain in a wakening day. Such adventures are without price, but they bring up the question of how safe it is not only for thirteen-year-old boys to camp by themselves in the desert, but for anyone. And the answer is, of course, that it is just as safe as you make it. With common sense and a knowledge of the special conditions and hazards the desert provides, it is as safe to sleep on a mountain slope or under a distant cactus as in one's own backyard. However, it might be added that with the increasing prevalence of man, it is no longer as safe as it once was.

The hazard of heat is most often associated with the desert, but actually many people are killed by cold. Often this is because the greenhorn in shirt sleeves will set out to climb a desert mountain in the warmth of a winter day, and on reaching higher elevations several hours later, will find himself in a blizzard. Water is another major cause of death, but too much of it rather than too little. Flash floods come sweeping down a dry river bed even if it hasn't rained in the immediate vicinity, hence a good rule of thumb is not to camp in a dry wash or canyon bottom.

If by chance a camper, or for that matter anyone, should find himself in the desert for longer than he bargained, as one might if one's car broke down on a deserted road, there are ways of keeping alive. During the hot weather it is important not to let oneself become dehydrated. Traveling should be done at night and in the cool of the day. During the hot hours one should rest under shade; that of a creosote will do, or of a saguaro if you're skinny. It is possible to obtain water from certain species of cactus, particularly the barrel cactus, by cutting into the plant with a knife or breaking it open with a rock so as to expose the firm white pulp. Pieces of this can be chewed which, though no lemon ice, will do a great deal to relieve thirst. As for food, cactus fruit can be eaten, and animals such as reptiles and rodents. The pack rat, like the porcupine, is a notable example of an animal that can be caught without special equipment. Its nest can easily be torn apart with

A pack rat's nest

a stick and the animal captured. Peter caught one just the other day this way, although in the process he was bitten. Also, says my husband, you might be lucky enough to find a rattlesnake in the pack rat's nest, which would give you a second course.

The wildlife, instead of being considered useful, is undoubtedly what most people imagine to be the greatest peril of all, a peril not at all confined just to camping trips. "Aren't you afraid to *live* out there, with all those things around that sting and bite?" I am often asked by Easterners. The traditional picture of the hazards to desert living begins with the inhabitant shaking out his shoes before putting them on in case a scorpion is hiding there, and after numerous encounters with rattlesnakes and Gila monsters, ends with him peering under his bed at night for a tarantula. As I have discussed earlier, the fauna is much more misunderstood than dangerous, and you learn to accept it and live with it much as the city dweller does the car-filled streets.

In fact, most of the elements considered to be dangerous to the camper are, to some degree, handicaps to desert living. The heat for some is a decidedly unpleasant factor, though air-conditioned houses, stores, and cars practically eliminate it unless you fancy taking long walks after lunch. Besides, a community needs a period of either hibernation or aestivation when the social wheels can slow down for a while. Here people withdraw into their houses to escape the heat as in wintry places they do to escape the cold.

Water is certainly a problem but, as with the camper, we are oddly enough plagued more by its occasional overabundance than by its scarcity, which has not yet become forcibly evident, though that day is fast approaching. Ours is not just a question of picnicking in the path of a flash flood, but of building a house. A heavy downpour will fill up the dry washes which Tucson's suburbs have so unconcernedly engulfed, the water sometimes spreading out to cover the flood plains or low areas immediately lining the washes. That this ever happens is almost impossible for those who have not seen it to believe, and so it is difficult to pass and enforce the necessary restrictions to prevent homes being built in the danger zones. The homeowner is unaware, and the developer is out to make money wherever he can.

Our potential water courses, crowded with mesquite and cottonwoods, make handsome natural green belts that can serve as much-needed "open areas" in the midst of the increasing urban sprawl. The farsighted planner keeps attempting to protect them from the subdivider and the engineer who dream of eliminating the trees and turning the washes into huge cement-lined ditches with houses crowded to their very edges.

Besides water, its lack or occasional excess, the dryness may be considered a handicap, though some of us boast of our low humidity that in spring and fall drops below ten per cent. What is good for the sinuses and arthritis is not at all helpful to the skin or naturally curly hair, but a large bottle of lotion and a hair spray will remedy the situation. Neither is our famous aridity at all good for lilacs or lilies of the valley. So, unless you wish to spend your days watering trees and plants, you give up trying to create a "little bit of New England" on the desert, and grow what the desert will best support.

A new exhibit at the Museum demonstrates how native plants can be incorporated into gardens for ornamental purposes as well as for the useful purpose of providing shade and saving water. A surprisingly wide variety of plants are available, ranging from the handsome mesquite and palo verde trees to shrubs such as the creosote, salt bush, and jojoba, down to the small flowering perennials like the zinnia and paper-flowers. A recent issue of *Sunset* Magazine listed almost thirty usable desert plants. The only truly nonirritating and pleasant way to live in the desert is to recognize its conditions and adapt one's life to them as have done its plants and animals.

From my housekeeping point of view, the dust is a much more annoying factor than the "varmints," dryness, and heat. In the months of March and April and again in October, the winds sweep across the desert, turning into dust bowls the bare places where the subdivider has scraped off the growth in preparation for the building of tract houses. These often lie vacant for long periods of time, and along with the unpaved roads, are responsible for most of our dust. But I try to remind myself that it's dust, not smog, though we are beginning to get some of that too. On certain days you can see long streamers of smoke pouring down several mountain passes from the smelter on the other side of the Catalinas, and on the city's outskirts the smoke stacks of several sand and gravel plants send out a blanket of gray to which the car fumes contribute their share. My husband often comments on how he can hardly see the city as he approaches it from the Museum, and the days that the mountains stand out clearly are decreasing rapidly.

But on the other side of the ledger, living in the desert has many advantages. We do not have to battle ice, sleet, or snow. We can hang up the wash on a June day and by the time we have finished, the first clothes are already dry. And where else can such interesting companions be found with whom to share one's house? Once we illustrated this in our Christmas card, which featured our version of Pandora's Box. In a large carton we placed the boys, the dog, the domestic cat, and two bobcats. Photographing this faunal assemblage proved almost impossible and after a harassing hour of assuaging tempers with lollipops, bits of meat, and doggie treats, of mopping candy-streaked boy faces, of retrieving huffy bobcats and an exuberant dog, my husband was near collapse. "Why," he moaned, "can't we just have a red petunia on our card like other people?" He meant a poinsettia.

*   *   *

This afternoon I watched the two older boys set out to see the red-tailed hawk's nest these birds have maintained for several years in the sycamore tree near our east fence. In his hand each held a saguaro rib for a staff and Peter, the oldest, was carrying the binoculars so they could spy on the birds if they were around. John carried a bagful of cookies and two apples. They were going by the way of the old Indian campground in hopes that the last rain would have uncovered more pottery and perhaps an arrowhead. As they went out the door they told me not to expect them back for several hours as they thought they would go lizard hunting with Frank and Alex, the oldest of a nearby Mexican family whose mother, without electricity or running water, manages to keep her large brood far cleaner than I do. Behind them as they disappeared over the hill trotted the dog and the wolf.

In many ways it is an insignificant thing to watch two boys set out on an afternoon's walk through the desert. They will follow a trail they have walked over many times. They will see the same bushes, the same trees, and hear the same birds. Yet this little vignette is increasingly significant as our Arizona desert is covered with houses or turned into irrigated fields. A new subdivision is already creeping up our road, and soon the city will have spread out so far that it will lap at the very flanks of the surrounding mountains. I wonder if our grandsons will be able to walk in the desert as our sons do, if my brother's grand-daughters will be able to walk in an eastern wood as do his daughters. I wonder how successful those few men will be throughout our nation who realize that the land is something to be cherished, something to be admired as well as used, something to be passed on to the future, and that if we destroy it, whether a forest or a desert or a river, we destroy much of what makes life worth living. More than that, we destroy the source of our inspiration. If we are to survive on the desert, the desert itself must survive. And so the problem of space is as acute as any.

How this can be answered in the years to come, with our tradition of depredation and under the pressures of creeping urbanization, is difficult to imagine. A park, such as New York's Central Park, would be considered an impossibility, a dream of madmen, were it not a fact. How does Tucson, a city of inadequate parks, view its many lost opportunities, if it views them at all? But though much here is too late, something is still possible, and a number of our citizens and public officials, by attempting to protect the natural green belts along the water courses from the developer and the engineer who wish to turn them into cement ditches, are making a beginning. The day might even come when an enlightened tax plan would encourage rather than penalize the holders of sizable acreage in the flood plains.

Unfortunately, the shortsightedness of those who could most easily do something keeps Tucson growing steadily uglier. We are still running the same old race between greed and ignorance on the one hand and on the other the slowly growing awareness of how vital to our well-being are parks and natural untouched areas within and close to our cities. Whenever I drive to the airport, my eyes scan without relief the sea of roofs, the unending asphalt, the tangle of telephone poles, neon signs, and billboards, and I do not understand how we can tolerate so much ugliness, or is it that we refuse to recognize the signs of our torment? Of course, the setting is still beautiful, with the girdling mountains and the desert. But give us a few more years and we shall have disposed of the desert, and with a bit more ingenuity I'm sure we can figure out how to do something useful with those mountains.

Our own immediate answer has been to buy enough land when it was still cheap so as to protect ourselves. With care we placed our house not on the top but on the side of our western hill where we are shielded from the wind and future neighbors and yet can look to the mountains. Here we are as unconscious of the man-made world as it is possible to be and still make use of its undoubted conveniences. It came as quite a surprise when I first realized that this was not everyone's heart's-desire. Sometimes I am asked why we didn't build on the hilltop so that we could see the lights of Tucson. But I guess I am secretive by nature, and, like Hadrian, at times want to pull up the hills around me to shut out the world. To survive we need solitude, or is it just I that need it?

A city-dwelling friend of mine once said to me, "Out there on the desert, you don't know what life is all about! Why, you're raising a bunch of ostriches!" If I had said that at least we did read, she would have laughed and expostulated about Experience. I worried about it for a while, thinking dubiously about her life: a round of "affairs," committee meetings, and intellectual cocktail parties where Life is fragmented into meaningless question marks and picked over until everyone drifts off to listen to progressive jazz in a consciously "mixed" all-night bar. I wondered at her children: if riding on subways, roller-skating with a neighborhood gang, and spending Saturday mornings at the movies or museums is any more the key to life than is the desert. "What life is all about," I have since learned, comprises the things that you yourself know and think important.

To my friend the stagnating mind is what tattletale gray is to the conscientious housewife. Because I live in the stillness of the desert, she thinks that inevitably I must sink into the mists of apathy, unaware of what is around me, unaware of myself. What gives her a sense of her own identity, of being alive, are the turbulent scenes of her own life: screaming in anger, writhing in lust, weeping in despair. Quietness to her is death. What she is searching for, I suppose, is intensity of experience; and it is so much easier to think you're really "living" by "living-it-up." Feeling guilty for the fact that she is not black, not poor, not crippled, not Clytemnestra, she takes the clay of her life and fashions out of it things that will cause her pain and humiliation. I cannot imagine, in the end, that it makes any difference how we are shaped, how the room is furnished. A hell can be anywhere, as the heart of the flame anywhere is the complexity and tortuousness of human relationships and human desires.

In her footsteps a social scientist, though he politely did not call us ostriches, asked me how I thought the boys' upbringing would affect them as adults: how they would respond to the slums and depressed masses, to the problems of conflicting races, to joining the army or a political party. "What do you think will become of them in the face of the increasing urbanization?" he further asked. I felt like shrugging and muttering an old family adage, "TWT," Time Will Tell, and that quite soon enough.

I should have answered that I do not so much care about what becomes of them as about what kind of men they will become. But naturally I am concerned over what becomes of them also, in a vague, unworded way, because as a mother I love them, and in some mysterious fashion they are part of my own imagined immortality. Yet as a mother I am also involved in the immediate problems and am not interested in speculating on made-up future ones.

That is not altogether true, for in the stillness of the night certain questions flutter restlessly in the caves of my mind. I think about ostriches. What troubles me about them is not so much their mythical head-burying propensities, but the fact that their

Michael and baby javelina

wings are too small to fly. Not to fly, forever earthbound, that indeed is terrible. Society says our sons are among the lucky ones with no congenital ostrich wings to impede their flight since their wings have sprouted white, Christian, and unmortgaged. But in the hour of full plumage will these same wings be strong, resilient and capable of sweeping them up into the clear cold air where they must question their society as well as the universe; and will they be able to fly steadily on with those questions always hovering about them? So again I ask myself about the desert. What does it teach?

John and badger

By learning to be at ease with the desert, have our sons learned to be at ease with themselves? Then, not bound by the need to constantly prove themselves, will they be able to reach out freely and unafraid to touch what brushes by them, to give of the heart and to receive? In accepting the final unknowability of the desert, perhaps they can accept the final unknowability of themselves and of those whom they love. And, confident that they can know as much of the desert as is necessary, so too can they know as much as is needed of themselves and others.

The desert, in fact the world of nature, because it is wholly impartial, is a teacher from whom children can learn spontaneously, without resentment. It is very simple. Should they step in cactus, get stung by a scorpion, be caught in a storm, fail to catch lizards, only they are to blame. Bad luck is in reality carelessness, faulty judgment, ignorance. As long as bad luck is used as an excuse, or even the labels that birth pins on us, we can never come to terms with ourselves. To do that we must assume the final responsibility of what we are and what we do. But, besides this, I hope the desert has taught our sons that they do not *own* the earth, that it is lent to them for as long as they treat it properly and respect the creatures with whom they share it.

Perforce this breeds a tenderheartedness that to some might seem unmanly. I remember the evening that Hugh watched on TV the concluding debacle in the movie *Moby Dick* where the boats were being smashed, the sailors tossed into a sea red with blood, and the whale was covered with harpoons and terrible wounds. Valiantly trying to see the best side of things, his sympathies all with Moby Dick, he said, "Well, salt water's good for cuts."

The desert wears many precious jewels among its thorns, and if we believe that there really are "sermons in stones" then we must defend our desert schoolroom with as much energy as we would the more formal one behind walls. In defending it we are also, obviously, defending our definition of the good life, even if it is only in front of a zoning board.

I suppose everyone of us is concerned, admittedly or not, with arriving at some definition of what is a good life so that we can live it, so that our children can. The unexamined life is of no more interest now than it was to Socrates, for what makes us different from a turtle is our awareness of ourselves, of our separateness, at once our curse and our glory. We stepped across the line, from animal innocence to recognition of self, a long time ago; and as we gazed about us with new-seeing eyes, we picked up a stone and scratched on a cave wall our wonder and our loneliness.

Charles Lamb saw the first man as a prisoner in the Garden who with Promethean courage sinned his way out of it—though perhaps his meaning is not altogether as I would have it. Being female, I see a small night-haunted boy setting out alone in the dark to join his brother who was looking for spadefoot toads down by the stream, because he too must see them. I see him walking resolutely and frightened along the moonlit path, careful not to glance on either side where the shadows are thick and whisper in his ear, nor yet behind him so that he wouldn't run and be called a 'fraidy-cat. I hear him call his brother's name, eager for another voice, and shout at him to look at the beautiful big moon, and I am filled with a smiling ache for all mankind which in its fear can still look at the moon and see its beauty.

Our definition of the good life would certainly not suit everyone, not because it is a desert with which we live, but nature. To some, nature is unessential, as only in man's world can they feel wholly sentient and alive. To others it is a fearsome thing. I once had a friend who sat nervously on the edge of our picnic, feeling threatened, and finally retreated to the house where nature could be looked at in small glances through protecting glass. Many others are like him, afraid that nature will rob them of their reason, for to them she is an irrational and malignant goddess out

to get them; and her servants, the animals, are lowly inferior creatures, the word "beastly" being one of censure. To them man,
made in the image of God, is still the pivot of the universe, with
the privilege of extinguishing the life of an animal or of a river.
To respect animals is to threaten man's dignity; to waste time in
defending them is to blaspheme against the works of Michelangelo,
Mozart, and Dante, and against the misery of the starving, the
sick, and the poor.

But the joke of it is, of course, that unless a man respects
other life, he won't respect human life, not even his own. Only
with that simple yet infinitely compassionate gesture of caring for
something different from himself can man display his humanity.
"The ancient values of dignity, beauty, and poetry which sustain
it [human life] are of Nature's inspiration: they are born of
the mystery and beauty of the world. Do not dishonour the earth
lest you dishonour the spirit of man" (Henry Beston).

I used the word "different," a word that today seems to have
become a value judgment. But "different" does not mean inferior
or superior, better or worse, it means simply—different, not the
same as. An animal is different from me, a man is different from a
woman, different from another man. It is this that gives us our
variety, our richness of texture, of sound, of meaning. I wonder
why we must measure everything by ourselves, and finding it
different, claim it is inferior. Of animals, Henry Beston said
"They are not brethren, they are not underlings; they are other
nations, caught with ourselves in the net of life and time, fellow
prisoners of the splendour and travail of the earth."

It would be cheating if I pretended that Rousseau's back-to-
nature-and-the-simple-life routine is the whole story. A child must
see both worlds, man's as well as nature's. When a child reads a
certain combination of words in a book, listens to a certain combination of sounds on a record or in a symphony hall, looks at
a certain combination of colors in a painting, the wonder that
out of man's mind has come such beauty will grow in him and

he will learn to honor man as well as nature, for how can he be whole unless he honors both?

It is so easy to make man too little. It is done every day in the name of realism. Out of these "truths" the clever fashion a miserable myopic creature crouched in the dust of his past, a whine in his throat. With bent head and twitching fingers he busily shreds his discontent and the world around him, unable to see the flashes of radiant beauty that rend his darkness and confusion. Can such a man honor anything, whether himself, the earth, or even God?

I pause to look out the open window to where the desert stretches almost unbroken to the closest mountains, and I watch a group of curious quail bobbing about in the mesquite tree as they try to look inside to where I am writing. Whenever I return to our small valley, bouncing up and down over the hills, I feel an inner ripple of gladness, and, like a dog shaking off water, I shake off the buzz of the city-hive I've left behind. Having swung like a pendulum between guilty indifference and a terrible awareness of what lurks behind the human mask, I return to myself. Here, in the calm, composed desert, I can alleviate the unscratchable internal itch brought on by current events and the social scene, by Bartók and Kandinsky; and it is here, in the natural world, whether of desert or woods or water, that I believe we find a vital sustenance, as an adult and as a child.

We are told that to be healthy we must have continuity. Well, then, we shall find it not only in man's past, but in the ordered rhythms and cycles outside our door: in the leaves falling from the trees and resprouting, in the seasonal rains, in the disappearance and return of the buzzards and the white-wings, in the death of the long-horned beetle after it lays its eggs, in the permanence of life itself rising like the phoenix out of the ashes of the individual.

As for form and order, do we not respond to the form and order that is evident in nature behind its seemingly endless variety and confusion? Where is form more precisely revealed than in a snowflake or a pollen grain? What is more harmonious than a

Beowulf and Michael

fading day, or, for that matter, nature's most ordinary face? If it is discipline that we admire, we have only to remember Voltaire's words, "Man is the only animal that drinks when he isn't thirsty and makes love all the year around."

"Alienated" is the cry of those who today claim not to have been lulled into apathy by our comfortable, soulless, materialistic society, but our unhappy and angry young men are not so much alienated from society as from themselves. Their inner chaos does not give birth to a dancing star, but to a long sad wail of self-pity. Ironically, this plaguing isolation is the price we paid for our dominion. When we stride across the earth we accept as natural the flight of whatever animal we surprise, unaware that this is the root of our unbearable loneliness, for what is more alienating than our neighbor's fear and mistrust? Then, when a bobcat rushes up to you from behind a bush purring loudly, and rubs against your legs, you feel an enormous elation, as if you have suddenly been reprieved. Together you sit on the hill watching the sun set,

and in the beat of both your hearts is the beat of all life since the beginning.

Inevitably we inflict on our children what we think is good for ourselves. Sweaters, says my husband, are what mothers make children wear when they themselves are cold. So I have had little difficulty in convincing myself that bringing up children—and this is what I am above all else concerned with—in a setting such as ours, is an effective preventive of alienation. Here each can come to be at one with himself as he becomes at one with what is outdoors. If we can feel part of the natural world, of the cycle of life, surely we will feel less isolated. Upon us then will fall the not-to-be-minimized blessing expressed in one of those contemporary cards depicting a tangle of snakes, and captioned, "Cheer

up, we're all in this together!" The birds, the bees, the flowers that
surround us provide just this kind of comfort. We are all in this
together, and they, for one, can show and incite joy. "Recreation,
pleasure, amusement, fun and all the rest are poor substitutes for
Joy; and Joy, so I at least am convinced, has its roots in something
from which civilization tends to cut us off" (Joseph Wood Krutch).

Nature holds up a mirror in which, if we care to look, we can
see ourselves in a vast scene, not lost but blended. A home is not
just a house; it is the natural world around it, and with both his
feet well rooted in this a child can look out with confidence to the
world of man. Each will then have its proper meaning and proportion. Our home is the desert, and from it will come identity,
solace and, yes, Joy, above all, Joy.